A *Discipled Nation* Series

OVERCOMING
Subtle Sins

The Key to
Dynamic
Discipleship

JIM DYET & JIM RUSSELL

A Discipled Nation Book®

The Amy Foundation, P.O. Box 16091, Lansing, Michigan 48901

ISBN 1-931744-25-4

Printed in the United States of America

CONTENTS

OVERCOMING Subtle Sins

PREFACE

Some of my neighbors seem to enjoy washing their cars. The bucket brigade swings into action every weekend. I haven't joined the brigade; I simply visit a drive-through car wash after every third or fourth gas fill-up. My car doesn't gleam like the neighbors' cars, but it looks respectably clean and I never feel soggy.

Of course, a drive-through car wash can't remove inside-window spots. They are solely my responsibility. I must identify them and get rid of them. If I don't, they will multiply, obscure my view, and perhaps cause an accident.

Like spots on the inside of car windows, subtle sins smudge the soul. Although our lives may appear clean on the outside, subtle sins are clearly visible to God.

What are some of these subtle sins? Pride is one. Jealousy is another. The list also includes, but isn't limited to, addiction, anger, animosity, anxiety, bitterness, boastfulness, closed-mindedness, covetousness, discouragement, dogmatism, fear, gluttony, gossip, hatred, haughtiness, idolatry, immoral fantasies, impatience, inflexibility, insincerity, irritability, judgmentalism, laziness, lukewarmness, lying, materialism, moodiness, negativism, prayerlessness, prejudice, resentment, rudeness, self-righteousness, selfishness, skepticism, unbelief, unforgiveness, ungratefulness, and vanity. These are the kinds of sins that lurk deep inside us and are ready at a moment's notice to spring forth like ravenous tigers released from cages. Unconfessed and unchecked, these sins disrupt our fellowship with God, damage our relationships, and destroy every opportunity to experience peace, joy, and spiritual productivity.

This book takes a hard, honest look at subtle sins. It exposes the hypocrisy behind them, strips away whatever excuses are offered for harboring them, and explains how to expunge them from our lives.

Following Jesus Christ allows no excursions into the paths of sin. The straight and narrow way—the way of righteousness—is the way Jesus leads. As the apostle John pointed out:

"We know that we have come to know him if we obey his commands. The man who says, 'I know him,' but does not do what he commands is a liar, and the truth is not in him. But if anyone obeys his word, God's love is truly made complete in him. This is how we know we are in him: Whoever claims to live in him must walk as Jesus did" (1 John 2:3-6).

—Jim Dyet

OVERCOMING Subtle Sins

PART ONE:

Identifying Subtle Sins

OVERCOMING Subtle Sins

Chapter 1

WHAT EXACTLY ARE SUBTLE SINS?

Ah, the joys of summer! Warm temperatures, bright sunshine, the smell of mown grass, the beauty of flower gardens, fresh fruits and vegetables, ice cream socials, picnics in the park, ball games, and restful days at the beach. What could be more perfect? How about warm temperatures without humidity, bright sunshine without sunburn, the smell of mown grass without allergies, the beauty of flower gardens without the threat of weeds, fresh fruits and vegetables without chemical sprays, ice cream socials without calories, picnics in the park without bees and ants, ball games without rain delays, and restful days at the beach without sand between your toes? But that is just wishful thinking. Nothing on earth is perfect—not even summer.

Not even human beings created in God's image!

According to the Bible, everyone has sinned (Romans 3:23). Fortunately, in spite of our sin God loves us and has provided forgiveness through His Son. Believers are forgiven but not perfect. This doesn't mean we have a *carte blanche* to sin; it means we have an obligation to avoid sin and to live in a way that honors God. As the apostle Paul indicated in Romans 6:2, " . . . we died to sin; how can we live in it any longer?"

Of course, most followers of Jesus lead a moral life. Our names stay off crime blotters, and our photos stay off post-office walls. We don't hold up fast-food restaurants or convenience stores. We don't deal drugs, snatch purses, or forge checks. All in all, we are law-abiding citizens, good neighbors, and churchgoers. But do we commit subtle sins—sins that aren't clearly visible as blatant sins are? Subtle sins operate insidiously. They may smolder in our hearts before they erupt in our actions. They may appear small, but they cause big damage to us and to others. Left unattended and unconfessed, they will smother our love for God, sap our spiritual vitality, and mock our claim that we are Jesus' followers.

Are we guilty of subtle sins? The response to this question depends upon how we answer the following questions. Do we tell a *lie* occasionally? Do we *gossip?* Are we *resentful* or *bitter? proud* or *impatient? rude* or *haughty? irritable* or *closed-minded? envious* or *jealous? prayerless* or *apathetic?* Do we *take God's goodness for granted? Can we identify someone we just can't stand?* Do we entertain *immoral fantasies?* Do we dismiss such traits as harmless or inevitable or just a part of human nature? If we answered yes to any or all of these questions, we are guilty of subtle sins, and we need to revisit Jesus' teachings.

Jesus taught that evil originates in the heart. It is not the product of a bad environment or a dysfunctional family or a below-poverty rating or the construction of one's genes or an inferior education. Jesus said, "For out of the heart come evil thoughts, murder, adultery, sexual immorality, theft, false testimony, slander" (Matthew 15:19). His words affirm what the prophet Jeremiah proclaimed to the nation Judah about 600 years earlier: "The heart is deceitful above all things . . . ." (Jeremiah 17:9). His teaching also recalls the Lord's indictment of the human race in the time of Noah: "The LORD saw how great man's wickedness on the earth had become and that every inclination of the thoughts of his heart was only evil all the time" (Genesis 6:5). Clearly, God knows our thoughts and emotions, and if they offend Him, we need to regard them as serious sins. They may be subtle, but they are as odious to God as murder and adultery.

Here's how Jesus characterized *some subtle sins:*

- He placed *spiteful anger* in the same category as murder. "You have heard that it was said to the people long ago, 'Do not murder, and anyone who murders will be subject to judgment.' But I tell you that anyone who is angry with his brother will be subject to judgment . . . " (Matthew 5:21, 22).

- He charged that *sexual lust* is a form of adultery. "You have heard that it was said, 'Do not commit adultery,' But I tell you that anyone who looks at a woman lustfully has already committed adultery with her in his heart" (Matthew 5:27, 28).

- He condemned a *vengeful attitude* (Matthew 5:38); *self-righteousness and hypocrisy* (6:1-5); *unforgiveness* (v. 15); *materialism* (vv. 19-24); *worry* (vv. 25-34); *judgmentalism* (7:1-5); *doubt, skepticism, and unbelief* (Mark 16:14; Luke 24:25; John 20:24-29); *selfish ambition* (Mark 10:35-45); *indifference* (Matthew 13:15; Luke 7:31-35); *lack of affection and ungratefulness* (Luke 7:40-47); *immoral fantasies and slander* (Matthew 15:19); *deception* (Mark 13:5); *fear* (John 14:27); *egoism and haughtiness* (Luke 14:7-11; 18:14b; 20:45); *discord and dissension* (John 6:43); and *prayerlessness* (Luke 22:45, 46).

Jesus' teachings about subtle sins underscore several truths. First, sin is sin whether it is covert or overt, visible to many or visible only to God. Second, we cannot legitimately excuse our subtle sins. The Lord does not accept such lame defenses as, "I am only human" or "Everybody has a bad day now and then" or "I can't help it; I was born that way" or "Sure, I have a hot temper; after all, I *am* a redhead." He holds us accountable for our unconfessed subtle sins as well as our blatant sins. Jesus warned: "There is nothing concealed that will not be disclosed, or hidden that will not be made known" (Luke 12:2). In his letter to the Romans, the apostle Paul reiterated Jesus' pronouncement. He wrote concerning future judgment: "This will take place on the day when God will judge men's secrets through Jesus Christ, as my gospel declares" (2:16).

A person may feel that smoldering resentment or bottled-up anger or egoism or immoral fantasies or covetousness or idolatry are locked deep inside. He assumes they are his secret cache of wrongs and has no intention of confessing and forsaking them. But just as every web site visited on a computer can be tracked on a hard drive, so every unconfessed subtle sin leaves its mark on the soul. Someday God will retrieve it and judge it!

Comparing ourselves with those whose sins seem larger than life may convince us that we live on higher moral ground and our subtle sins are nothing to be concerned about. Criminals and nasty neighbors deserve condemnation. On the other hand, we deserve commendation. Criminals and nasty neighbors are the bad guys. They wear black hats. We're the good guys. We wear white hats. We reason that we have favored-class status with God.

A proud father and mother attending Parents Day at a military academy watched the cadets parade past them and hundreds of other parents. Catching sight of her son, the mother pulled on her husband's shirt sleeve. "Look, Dear," she blurted, "everyone's out of step but our son Jimmy."

Are we like Jimmy's parents? Even when the Bible parades our subtle sins past us, do we fail to see that we are woefully out of step with God's will? Others may see our egoism or irritability or anxiety or judgmentalism or skepticism, but we may not see it because we choose not to. Sadly, we will never experience the blessings and joy God wants to give us until we see our subtle sins as God and others see them and repent.

Robert Burns, the revered 18th-century Scottish poet, must have understood the significance of viewing ourselves from a more reliable perspective than our own. He wrote:

> *Oh would some power the giftie gie us*
> *To see ourselves as others see us.*

The King James Version uses the words "sincere" and "without offence" in Philippians 1:10 to describe what kind of people believers ought to be. *The New International Version* uses the words "pure" and "blameless." Both translations are based on the Greek word *eilikrineis* derived from the words for "sun" and "to judge." Therefore, it indicates the purity of a substance or object that is tested by sunlight. Clearly, *eilikrineis* provides clear notification that our character, as well as our conduct, must bear God's presence and activity. We are, after all, His workmanship (Ephesians 2:10).

Have you known anyone who purchased a "previously owned" car, only to learn later that its outward shine betrayed a faulty engine or transmission? More than a few first-century consumers experienced a similar fate at the hands of crafty, unscrupulous, merchants who hid the cracks in their pottery by filling them with wax and coloring over the defective areas. After purchasing a doctored piece of pottery and setting it outdoors, a buyer soon discovered he or she had been deceived. Strong sunlight would melt the wax and reveal the vessel's cracks.

Fortunately, honest craftsmen could be found in the first century, just as honest car salesmen can be found today. Many honest first-century pottery vendors placed signs at their marketplace stalls, advertising in Latin: *sine cera*, "without wax." Our English word "sincere" comes from *sine cera.* If we are sincere, as Philippians 1:10 instructs, God's workmanship will be clear to all. There will be no bad surprises!

Philippians 1:10 also summons us to be "without offence" (KJV) or "blameless" (NIV). The Greek word is *aproskopoi,* meaning *not causing anyone to stumble.* The same word appears in 1 Corinthians 10:32, where we read, "Do not cause anyone to stumble."

Can a subtle sin like discord cause anyone to stumble? In answer to this question think of the damage discord has inflicted on more than a few professing believers. Some refuse to get involved at church because of the "politics" there. Others have stopped attending church altogether, because they grew tired of seeing Henry snub Bill because Bill's choice of a color scheme for the church offices clashed with his; or they became exasperated because church members bickered over items in the church budget or over worship styles.

No, it doesn't take an act of adultery on the part of a church leader to cause someone to stumble. Nor does it take an act of embezzlement on the part of the church treasurer to weaken the faith of the faithful. Any number of subtle sins can trip and injure those who are trying to walk along the straight and narrow road.

After hearing glowing reports of the Welsh Revival, an American believer traveled to Wales to investigate the phenomenon. He approached a police constable in the first city he visited and asked, "Officer, can you tell me where the revival is?"

The constable put a finger on one of the shiny buttons on his uniform jacket and replied, "Under these buttons, sir."

Revival is always an individual matter. When it reaches the heart, subtle sins flee; then blessings and joy move in and overflow to family, congregation, and community.

For Personal Reflection and/or Group Discussion

1. Why do you agree or disagree that subtle sins are just little, unimportant sins?

2. If God convicted someone of subtle sins, how should that person respond? If He convicted your congregation of subtle sins, how do you think your congregation would respond? Why?

3. If you were to compare the spiritual condition of the human heart to a color, what color would you choose? Why?

4. How can a believer help another believer cope with subtle sins?

5. How do subtle sins manifest themselves in family living? How can families learn obedience to Jesus' teachings?

6. What link, if any, do you see between discipling oneself and discipling our nation?

7. What do you believe are the three most frequently committed subtle sins?

8. How can obeying Jesus' teachings help His followers overcome anger, hatred, prejudice, and resentment?

9. What might a place of employment be like if the employer were an obedient follower of Jesus? If the employees were obedient followers of Jesus?

10. How might a righteous life persuade others to be obedient followers of Jesus?

Chapter 2

PRIDE GOES BEFORE A FALL

If you are an American, your eyes probably get misty and your heart beats faster when you hear Lee Greenwood's patriotic song, "God Bless the U.S.A." General Norman Schwarzkopf prized this song so highly that he used it as the anthem for Desert Storm in the Persian Gulf War.

The refrain alone speaks volumes:

> I'm proud to be an American
> where at least I know I'm free,
> And I won't forget the men who died
> who gave that right to me,
> And I gladly stand up next to you
> and defend her still today,
> 'Cause there ain't no doubt I love this land.
> God bless the U.S.A.

Such pride of country is admirable. Although America has its faults and needs to recognize God as its benefactor and guide, its reputation for compassion, prosperity, peace, and opportunity is unrivaled. "One nation under God," is the best nation on earth!

Pride of accomplishment is honorable too. It's what drives our economy and leads to ingenious technological advances. Who would want a heart surgeon to operate on a loved one if that surgeon didn't care whether he succeeded or not? What kind of work would a plumber leave behind if he didn't have pride of accomplishment? How many widgets would an assembly line produce if workers along the line had no pride of accomplishment? Studies have shown that when a team of assembly line workers posts the number of widgets it produced on its shift, the next shift of workers does as well or better. The power of pride of accomplishment!

Family pride is honorable too. Some bumper stickers announce "Proud Parent of a Jenkins Middle School Student" or "My Kid Excels at Lincoln High" or "My Daughter Won First Place in

Baton Twirling."

What, if anything, makes some forms of pride sinful—even obnoxious?

Pride crosses the line and becomes sinful when it is self-serving. A person with sinful pride puts himself on a pedestal. He believes he is better than others, deserves their admiration, and covets their praise. He rejects the notion that he should acknowledge God and be grateful to Him.

Pride of country is good if we acknowledge that God has blessed this great land. It is sinful if we take all the credit to ourselves and look down our noses at other countries. Pride of family is good, but it is sinful if a parent harps about how well daughter Heather plays the harp. It is sinful if we flaunt our fortunes or tout our talents or sing our own praises or expect special treatment because we think we are special or better than others.

The Bible uncovers many cases of sinful pride from the dawning of human history to the end of time. The first episode involved Lucifer, commonly called the devil or Satan. He began his existence as a highly privileged angel. God had granted him a place near His throne. The name Lucifer means "light-bearer." He was a brilliant creature of dazzling beauty. Isaiah 14:12 calls him "morning star" and "son of the dawn." Ezekiel wrote that "every precious stone adorned" him and his "settings and mountings were made of gold" (Ezekiel 28:13). He wrote further that he was "anointed as a guardian cherub . . . on the holy mount of God" (v. 14). But Lucifer's stellar career and glory were cut short. God cast him down from heaven to the earth. He fell from lofty privilege to lasting perdition, from proximity to God to opposition to God, from splendor to shame, from beauty to baseness, and from the delights of heaven to the doom of hell.

What caused such calamity? Ezekiel chalked it up to pride (28:17). Isaiah traced it to selfish ambition or what we might call an over inflated ego. Lucifer got too big for his cherubic shoes! He aspired to seize God's throne. He struck "worshiping God" from his to-do list and inserted "to be worshiped as God." He went so far as to lead one third of the angels in a rebellion against God (Revelation 12:3, 4). But his diabolical plan backfired. He learned what so many anti-God, power-hungry, bellicose dictators have also learned: No one can topple God from His throne.

Isaiah's account of Lucifer's fall provides an up-close look at the event. He wrote:

> "How have you fallen from heaven, O morning star, son of the dawn! You have been cast down to the earth, you who once laid low the nations! You said in your heart, 'I will ascend to heaven; I will raise my throne above the stars of God; I will sit enthroned on the mount of the assembly, on the utmost heights of the sacred mountain. I will ascend above the tops of the clouds; I will make myself like the Most High.' But you have been brought down to the grave, to the depths of the pit" (Isaiah 14:12-15).

Jesus, too, reported Lucifer's fall. He underscored its swiftness: "I saw Satan fall like lightning from heaven" (Luke 10:18).

At the end of time, proud Satan will still be trying to usurp God. Motivated by selfish ambition, he will marshal a vast army of unbelievers to battle the Lord and His people. However, the Lord will incinerate Satan's forces and cast Satan into the Lake of Fire (see Psalm 2 and Revelation 20:7-10).

No one should assume that *pride, ego,* and *selfish ambition* will escape God's judgment. He detects and detests *these subtle sins,* cancers of the heart that spread and destroy the potential for a healthy relationship with Him and others. The timing of His judgment may be unknown, but its inevitability and swiftness are certain. Proverbs 16:18 teaches that pride precedes destruction and a haughty spirit goes before a fall.

Didn't Eve fall under divine judgment because of pride and selfish ambition? Satan tempted her to eat the only fruit God had placed off-limits in the Garden of Eden. He told her she would be like God if she ate the fruit. This prospect struck her pride and selfish ambition dead center. Why not partake of it? It looked wonderful. She was sure it would taste as good as it looked and would make her wise like God. So she succumbed to the temptation, gobbled up some of the fruit and gave some to her husband Adam. Twang! The spring on the trap Satan had set closed instantly, locking Adam and Eve into sin and judgment. Just as God had predicted, they fell under the sentence of death (Genesis 2:17; 3:19; Romans 5:12). For the first time in their lives, they found themselves separated from God, plagued with guilt, and facing imminent expulsion from Paradise (Genesis 3:7-10, 22-24).

Pride, egoism, and *selfish ambition* have carved an ugly trail through history. These subtle sins did not leave the human race when Adam and Eve, our first parents, left the Garden of Eden. Many have walked that trail and discovered that it leads to a bitter end. Even a few prophets, apostles, and preachers have followed it. Much to their shame and remorse they have experienced the harm pride causes.

The Hanging Gardens of Babylon are one of the Seven Wonders of the World, but a long time ago a wonder of a different kind took place in Babylon. God transformed powerful and proud King Nebuchadnezzar into a wild man stripped of glory and authority and driven by his subjects into isolation, where wild animals roamed and he ate grass like cattle.

It happened when Nebuchadnezzar was strutting on his palace roof. With chest expanded, chin stuck out, and nose lifted high, he asked, "Is not this the great Babylon I have built as the royal residence, by my mighty power and for the glory of my majesty?" (Daniel 4:30). The words were still on his lips when a voice from heaven sentenced him to seven years away from his kingdom and into the wild animal kingdom. Nebuchadnezzar would learn the hard way that God judges pride and boastfulness and that He alone is the sovereign Lord of life (vv. 31, 32).

None of us followers of Jesus resemble Nebuchadnezzar, do we? We wouldn't dream of climbing onto a rooftop and boasting that we built our better homes and gardens by our mighty power and for the glory of our majesty. But does the Nebuchadnezzar virus exist in our blood? Isn't it sinful pride that prompts us to drop names, to boast about our career accomplishments, to mention our expensive "toys," and to list our vacation trips to exotic places? Instead of humbly acknowledging God's goodness, do we credit our own intelligence, skill, and hard work as the keys to our success?

Whether pride, egoism, and selfish ambition show in our actions or fester in our thinking, they offend God and await either our confession or His discipline. Even some well-known heroes of the faith in Bible times were guilty of the subtle sins of pride, egoism, and selfish ambition. Their experiences serve as clear warnings to us.

Elijah demonstrated enormous faith at Mount Carmel by standing alone for God against 450 false prophets. Later, however, when wicked Queen Jezebel threatened his life, he fled to the Sinai desert, where he asked God to end his life (a senseless request, because if he had not fled, Jezebel would have gladly accommodated his death wish). He based his request on the fact that he was no better than his ancestors (1 Kings 19:4). Apparently, until his lapse of faith shown by his fear of Jezebel, he must have considered himself to be better than his ancestors. The subtle sin of pride had lodged in his heart. It stirred again in the desert, when Elijah boasted about his unblemished record of service to the Lord and set himself above the rest of his countrymen (vv. 10, 14). Only a fresh revelation of God's power and restoring grace took Elijah's focus off himself, placed it on God, plucked him from the desert, and set him on the path of service again.

Every believer bears a striking emotional resemblance to Elijah, according to James 5:17. Therefore, we should not be surprised if pride nestles in our hearts. It lurks in the feelings of the Sunday school teacher who looks down on those who refuse to enlist in their church's educational program. It skulks in the thinking of the 14-year-old boy who has memorized the Book of Romans and makes sure everyone knows about it. It rests in the attitudes of the soloist with the golden voice who loves the applause that follows her singing. Such proud attitudes ruin what could be sterling examples of Christian service and devotion to the Lord. If we allow pride to divert our focus from the Lord and lock it onto ourselves by calling attention to our "service" or ability, we divest ourselves of the rewards the Lord grants for humble, faithful service performed for His glory. Like Elijah, we need to refocus on our Lord!

The disciple Peter must have been likable most of the time. He exhibited leadership qualities and others seemed to be drawn to him. He was always in the thick of things, active, and talkative. But Peter demonstrated pride at times. En route to the Mount of Olives Jesus announced that all the disciples would desert Him, but Peter boasted that he would never do so (Matthew 26:31, 33).

"I tell you the truth," Jesus announced to Peter, "this very night, before the rooster crows, you will disown me three times" (v. 34).

Recoiling from the impact of Jesus' prediction, Peter boasted, "Even if I have to die with you, I will never disown you" (v. 35). Then the other disciples made the same boast.

Soon Peter learned it doesn't pay to boast. When temple guards arrested Jesus, Peter followed from a distance. The entourage went directly to the house of Caiaphas the high priest, where the Sanhedrin, the Jews' ruling body, had gathered to subject Jesus to a kangaroo trial, insults, and a beating. Peter stood in the courtyard. Warming himself by a fire, Peter denied three times that he knew Jesus. Later, he deeply regretted his turncoat behavior and was restored to fellowship with his risen Lord by the power of Jesus' love and forgiveness (see Matthew 26:75 and John 21:15-19).

This episode from Peter's life testifies to the impropriety of holding too high an opinion of oneself. The higher the platform we build for pride and self-confidence, the greater the risk of tumbling far and landing hard. The apostle Paul cautioned, " . . . if you think you are standing firm, be careful that you don't fall" (1 Corinthians 10:12).

Millions of moviegoers crowded theaters to see Titanic. History recalls that pride and overconfidence accompanied the launching of that famous ship. Her elegance, accommodations, and onboard entertainment were features to brag about. So were her double bulkhead doors. If ever a ship were seaworthy and secure, it was the Titanic. None of the passengers or crew were prepared for the calamity that occurred when the Titanic rammed a massive iceberg. Pride and overconfidence preceded Titanic's sinking and a watery grave.

Selfish ambition is a kissing cousin to sinful pride, as we learn from an encounter between Jesus and His disciples. During His earthly ministry, He taught His disciples many truths, including the really big truths that He would die for their sins and ours, be buried, rise again, ascend to His Heavenly Father, and return to earth to judge and to rule as King. The disciples snatched onto the fact that Jesus will establish His kingdom on earth, but they skipped right over what He said about dying. After all, they were Jews, and the Jews longed for a Messiah who would end the Roman occupation of Palestine and set up a Jewish kingdom. Even after

Jesus died and rose from the dead, the disciples asked Him: "Lord, are you at this time going to restore the kingdom to Israel?" (Acts 1:6). They had a bad case of chronic kingdomitis!

Once, after Jesus had predicted His death, two disciples—brothers James and John—asked Him to grant whatever they requested.

"What do you want me to do for you?" Jesus asked (Mark 10:36).

How would modern disciples answer Jesus' open-ended question? Would many ask for a job promotion with a big raise? a vacation away from the kids? a new house with a swimming pool? a Corvette? a scratch golf handicap? perfect teeth? James and John asked Jesus for second-in-command positions in His kingdom. They wanted to sit at his right and left.

Selfish ambition and egoism motivated James and John to make their outlandish request. But their mother, too, had her eye on these top positions for her sons (Matthew 20:20, 21). We can't fault a mother for wanting what she believes is best for her sons or daughters, but a truly wise mother wants what the Lord deems best for them.

Jesus' response to James and John crushes pride, egoism, and selfish ambition. He told them that pagan rulers grasp for political power so they can dominate others, but whoever wants to be great must serve others and whoever wants to be first must be everyone' slave (Mark 10:43). Further, He explained that He had not come to earth to be served but to serve and "to give his life a ransom for many" (v. 45).

The apostle John described a prominent church member who was so full of pride that he tried to dominate—to force his will on the rest of the congregation. "Diotrephes . . . loves to be first," John declared (3 John 9). Diotrephes had rejected John, the apostle of love, and was gossiping about him. Also, he would not welcome "the brothers" into the congregation. He even went so far as to excommunicate those who wanted to spread a welcome mat for the brothers (v. 10).

What a contrast to Diotrephes the description of Gaius presents! As members of the same congregation, both men should have patterned their lives after Jesus, but only Gaius did so. John described Gaius as a follower of Jesus who was faithful to the truth and walked continually in it (v. 3).

It seems every congregation has both a Gaius and a Diotrephes.

The Gaius type exudes love for Jesus and others. His humility and discipling ministry foster peace and harmony throughout the congregation. However, the Diotrephes type shows a lack of love for Jesus and others. Instead of serving the Lord, he acts as lord. He imposes his will on others, basks in the glow of the spotlight, and thinks he is indispensable. Those who disagree with him are told, "It's either my way or the highway."

A Diotrephes type in an Eastern state was accustomed to having his way. He wrote the church constitution and told everyone what to do—at church and at home. People were made to feel inferior and inadequate if they did not organize their lives and families according to his blueprints. He and his family sat directly front and center of the pulpit every Sunday until . . .

. . . the Sunday after a business meeting in which the members outvoted him. A motion passed that guaranteed missionary speakers a minimum honorarium, not just the amount received in a freewill offering. Every subsequent Sunday "Diotrephes" and his family huddled in a far corner of the sanctuary and refused to participate in the offering. Eventually his scowl and bitter words disrupted the fellowship of that congregation.

How serious is the subtle sin of pride? Very serious according to the following Scriptures:

> Psalm 101:5 warns that God will not endure "whoever has haughty eyes and a proud heart."
>
> Proverbs 6:16 and 17 announce that God hates "haughty eyes."
>
> Proverbs 11:2 states that "when pride comes, then comes disgrace."
>
> Proverbs 29:23 predicts that "a man's pride brings him low."
>
> Second Timothy 3:1-5 includes pride in a rogues gallery of sins that characterize the end times.
>
> James 4:6 teaches that "God opposes the proud."

Clearly, when pride gets the best of us, it reveals the worst of us, but there is hope. The Bible not only diagnoses *the subtle sins of pride, egoism, selfish ambition, and boastfulness,* but also prescribes a fail-proof cure. James 4:6b, the Lord extends grace to the humble. He urges the proud to submit themselves to Him, come near to Him, and receive the cleansing repentance brings. He promises to "give grace to the humble" (James 4:6) and invites: "Humble yourselves before the Lord, and he will lift you up" (James 4:10).

Jesus told about a Pharisee and a tax collector who entered the temple in Jerusalem to pray (see Luke 18:9-14). The Pharisee, obsessed with himself, offered God a list of his religious deeds. We can imagine that his pride of accomplishment made his head so big that it rattled the phylactery on his forehead! He thanked God that he was not like other men—robbers, evildoers, or adulterers—or even like the tax collector. He boasted that he fasted twice a week and tithed. The tax collector, on the other hand, was intent on finding God's forgiveness. He could not point to a list of religious good deeds, but he could point to a contrite heart. He pounded his chest and prayed, "God, have mercy on me a sinner."

Jesus said the repentant tax collector, not the proud Pharisee, received forgiveness. He explained, "For everyone who exalts himself will be humbled, and he who humbles himself will be exalted" (v. 14).

It seems the Lord places His greatest blessings on the lowest shelves. All who bend low before Him in repentance and humility receive those blessings.

Just a few decades ago most Americans shared Judeo-Christian values. Citizens showed respect for God and His Word. Traditional marriage and family life were valued. It was generally assumed that God was watching over the nation—protecting and blessing her. Television programming offered wholesome entertainment. Schools called Christmas programs "Christmas programs." "Merry Christmas" greetings far outnumbered "Happy Holidays" greetings. Drug traffic moved at a snail's pace. There were no Drug-Free Zone signs near schools. Road rage was almost unheard of. And love of country included respect for the flag and respect for those who fought and died to keep it flying. Today, however, the picture is alarmingly different. Widespread self-centeredness and pride have draped themselves over the land. The popular mood seems to be swinging away from God and country. Secularism and humanism reign as gods over many souls. Violence, profanity, and illicit sex flow through television channels and enter many homes. Drugs are readily available, even to grade-school kids. Patriotism and love for God are often identified as evidence of bigotry. We are encouraged to think globally and eclectically. Rampant pride and rejection of God may have our nation on a collision course with disaster.

How can concerned Americans launch a rescue operation? The answer lies in the fact that God can use men and women who have repented of sinful pride, egoism, and selfish ambition to rescue and restore America by discipling themselves and others. His blessings can extend from His obedient followers to their family members, their congregations, communities, and to the entire nation.

For Personal Reflection and/or Group Discussion

1. When does personal pride cross the line and become a subtle sin?

2. What reasons do followers of Jesus have to be humble?

3. How can an entry-level employee be career-conscious without committing the subtle sin of selfish ambition?

4. Why would you agree or disagree that "good guys finish last"?

5. Why do you agree or disagree that the subtle sin of egoism threatens marriages?

6. What do you think it means to humble yourself before the Lord?

7. How might even one's prayers reflect selfish ambition?

8. How can humility strengthen one's leadership?

9. How can humility strengthen family life?

10. How can humility strengthen congregational life?

Chapter 3

WHAT'S SO BAD ABOUT LOOKING OUT FOR NUMBER #1?

Older senior citizens remember the ice box and their parents' buying blocks of ice to put into it. They also recall Saturday nights, when the family sat quietly in the living room and listened to "shows" on a crackling radio. Fibber McGee and Molly, Jack Benny, the Great Gildersleeve, Amos 'n Andy, Fred Allen, George and Gracie, and the Green Hornet were regular radio entertainers. Popcorn was prepared in a screen basket held over a stove burner. In some homes the stove was fueled by wood or coal.

Sunday mornings, Dad cranked the car's engine or pushed the starter located under the accelerator, and the family drove to church. The rest of the day was usually quiet. Shopping could wait until Monday. Most stores were closed anyhow. After all, Sunday was the Lord's Day, a day of rest and worship.

Perhaps a number of senior citizens would like to reinstitute the Sundays of their childhood, but likely none would want to trade in their refrigerator for an ice box or their TV for a crackling radio or their microwave for a screen basket? And what would Sunday afternoon be like without football games shown on a big-screen TV from every possible angle and with instant replay? If church attendance is a family tradition, the family may drive two or three separate cars to get there.

We have come a long way in the past 60+ years, haven't we?

Or have we?

Has the proliferation of material possessions helped or hurt us? Do we control our things, or do they control us? What does it take to satisfy the heart? Just a little more?

King David's son Solomon lends some insight into these questions. For a while he engaged in a vigorous search for meaning and satisfaction. He tried education, work, wine, women, song, wealth, and possessions. However, he found neither significance nor satisfaction in these pursuits. He wrote concerning wealth and material possessions:

> "Whoever loves money never has money enough; whoever loves wealth is never satisfied with his income. This too is meaningless. As goods increase, so do those who consume them. And what benefit are they to the owner except to feast his eyes on them?" (Ecclesiastes 5:10, 11).

Solomon observed that every human being is born naked and takes nothing with him when he dies (v. 15). If God grants us wealth and possessions, we should enjoy them as His gifts, Solomon counseled (v. 19). He had come to understand that material things are temporary, whereas human beings live beyond their last breath. It is wise, therefore, to invest one's life for eternity than to spend it chasing after gold and gadgets. Life's true significance has God, not possessions, at its center. Therefore Solomon instructed: "Remember your Creator in the days of your youth" (Ecclesiastes 12:1), and "Fear God and keep his commandments, for this is the whole duty of man" (v. 13).

Years from now, people will be reminiscing about the popular TV show, "Who Wants to Be a Millionaire?" Easy question, isn't it? Who, other than a billionaire, doesn't want to be a millionaire?

If you are familiar with the "Millionaire" show, you probably remember some contestants who could have walked away with $125,000 or more but chose to continue in the game and lost all but $32,000 on a guess. Who can judge whether any of those contestants were greedy materialists? Chances are good, though, that greed played a part in some of the choices.

The subtle sin of greed feeds on materialism in life as well as on TV game shows. A greedy person may ruin his health in the dogged, singleminded pursuit of wealth and possessions. He may also lose his marriage. Worse, he may lose the opportunity to enjoy a good relationship with God and the opportunity to influence others to believe.

Jesus spoke about such a person and the folly of setting one's heart on material things. "A man's life does not consist in the abundance of his possessions," He remarked (Luke 12:15). To emphasize this truth, He mentioned a prosperous farmer who planned to demolish his barns to make room for bigger ones. Looking at a bumper crop, the farmer assured himself that he had "plenty of good things" put aside for many years. "Take life easy; eat, drink, and be merry," he advised himself (verse 19). However, something upset his plans permanently. Before the light of dawn swept over his fields, his soul was swept into eternity. By storing up things to the neglect of attention to God, the farmer had stored up judgment upon his soul (vv. 20, 21).

So, must a follower of Jesus live in a hovel to be holy? Is the great American dream diabolical? Must we treat possessions as poisons? Is it wrong to be rich but right to be poor? Will we be blessed if we bury our belongings, burn our bonds, scrap our stocks, cancel our bank accounts, abandon our homes, curse capitalism, and take vows of poverty? No. *The subtle sin of materialism* has everything to do with attitude and nothing to do with assets. Materialism assumes that money and possessions give true value to life. However, someone with very few possessions and a meager paycheck may be materialistic because he or she craves money and possessions, whereas someone who lives in an expensive house at the top of the hill, earns top dollar, and drives a top-of-the-line luxury car may be totally clear of materialism. Attitude makes the difference.

A TV preacher told his viewing audience that, because the Lord answers prayer, He would give a brand-new car to every viewer who had the faith to ask for one. Later, when some listeners wrote, telling the preacher they had been praying for weeks for a new car but still didn't have one, the preacher offered the following explanation: "God will not give you a new car until your prayers are very specific and you are obsessed with the car you want. Go to a dealer's showroom, obtain a brochure with pictures of the car you want, decide the options you want, and display a picture of the car in a prominent place in your home. Look at the picture many times throughout the day. Lock an image of it into your mind. Repeat over and over, 'I must have this car. I must have this car.' When you pray, tell God the make and model and every option you want on it."

How flawed is that thinking? Owning an affordable new car with a variety of options is fine, but letting the desire to own one command your waking moments is nothing but materialistic lust.

About 350,000 churches exist in the United States. They differ according to denominational labels, architecture, size, and location, but they have one thing in common. Their alleged purpose is to help people worship and serve God. It is a noble purpose that requires dedication, persistence, faith, and carefully prepared and dispensed servings of Jesus' teachings.

Jesus taught that no one can serve "both God and Money" (Matthew 6:24). It is inappropriate, therefore, to make money our master. Loved ones, friends, co-workers, and neighbors can learn from obedient followers of Jesus that serving God is truly fulfilling and far superior to serving money. They can be attracted to the Savior by seeing peace, contentment, a sense of purpose, and joy in the lives of those who heed what Jesus taught about true wealth. A willingness to accept this discipleship challenge could revolutionize our homes, our neighborhoods, and our nation.

The subtle sin of selfishness is closely allied with materialism. Selfish individuals are takers, not givers. Selfish spouses spend money for what *they* want. Jerry bought a boat for his fishing trips without consulting his wife Rose, but he blew a fuse when Rose purchased a small decorative basket at a house party. Rose's neighbor Brittany doesn't have an income of her own, but she and her husband budget a weekly allowance for each of them. Nevertheless, Rose wants more spending money for herself than she and her husband have agreed upon. And she has devised a scheme to get it. Whenever she shops at a grocery store, she pays by check. However, she writes the check for $50 more than the actual cost of the groceries and receives the difference in cash. Her husband hasn't caught on, but if he does . . . !

Marriage counselors report that the issue of money tops the list of reasons for divorce. Often, dissatisfaction with what a couple has drives them to acquire more, even if they have to stretch plastic money beyond its limits. They sign their lives away to purchase a state of the art home entertainment unit, a late-model SUV, high-tech exercise equipment, and a hot tub, etc., etc.. Soon, they have a house and a garage full of things, but they don't have a home. When the bills come due, they argue about whose idea it was to purchase "all this stuff," and they ask, "How will we ever pay these bills?" When the smoke has cleared, the bills are still on the table—alongside the divorce papers.

There may be some credence to the story about a woman who

sued her husband for religious reasons. She worshiped money, and he didn't have any.

Of course, the appeal of slick advertisements to consumers' materialistic attitude and selfishness contributes to personal debt and frustration. "Others may have turned you down for a loan because of bad credit," one TV commercial suggests, "but we will lend you the money you need so you can buy the car you need and deserve!"

Another commercial persuades couples to let their charge card whisk them away to a tropical island, where they can leave the workplace and its stress far behind. The commercial mentions nothing about the stress they will experience when they return home and find an enormous charge card bill sitting in their mailbox.

Apparently, credit card abuse is a major problem. According to a report in the *New York Daily News,* dated August 1, 1991, American consumers' credit card debt topped $700 billion, almost triple what it was in 1991. The average American household's credit card debt reached $8,123, up from $3,223 in 1991.

It is impossible to judge how much selfishness lies at the base of credit card debt. Credit cards may be flashed often to purchase gifts for loved ones and friends, especially at Christmas time; but surely selfishness drives many consumers to impulse buying. At such times the credit card seems to spring automatically from a billfold or purse and lands on a clerk's counter. *"Veni, vidi, Visa*—I came, I saw, I charged!"

Selfishness can cause even greater harm than plunging individuals into alarming debt. It has sapped love from marriages and families. Some mothers have left their husband and children in the lurch so they can "think of myself for a change" or "fulfill myself." It is not unusual for a woman in such cases to say she needs to "find herself," carve out her own career, and enjoy a sense of independence. And who hasn't heard of a marriage breaking up after 30 years because the husband has found a younger woman who flatters him (and takes his money)? We are no longer surprised to learn that a mother has deserted her husband and their young teens because she has grown tired of her domestic role.

A growing number of TV programs showcase selfishness. Their popularity seems to indicate that viewers relate well to the desire to serve self, even if it requires hurting others. The message is survive and win a fortune by any and all means. Vote others out of the running. Betray even those who think you are their friend. Outwit others. Set them up for a fall. Be the last one standing. It's all about oneself and the money!

How much better life is for married couples and single adults, too, who apply Jesus' teachings to their lives! They learn that it is "more blessed to give than to receive" (Acts 20:35). By putting the needs of others first, they not only help others but also experience personal benefits. The Lord gives them a sense of His presence, His peace, and His joy. Jesus always gives far more than we give to others in His name. Our bread cast on the waters seems to come back to us toasted, buttered, and covered with jelly.

All four Gospels relate the story of the Feeding of the Five Thousand. This famous story reveals several significant facts about Jesus: (1) He cares deeply about human need. He raised the subject of providing food for the multitude that followed Him (John 6:5). (2) He is the Son of God. His divine power enabled Him to turn two sardine like fish and five little bread rolls into a satisfying, all-you-can-eat meal for more than 5,000 people (vv. 8-11). (3) He richly rewards those who obey Him by putting the needs of others ahead of their own. After the 12 disciples had distributed the food and the people had feasted to their satisfaction, they followed Jesus' command to gather the leftovers. The tally of leftovers was 12 baskets (v. 13).

Twelve baskets and 12 disciples. Coincidence? Hardly. Undoubtedly, Jesus had planned for each disciple to enjoy a basket of food as a reward for faithful service to others.

When President George Bush, Jr. introduced his plan to help faith-based organizations assist the poor and needy, some perceived it as a violation of church and state. However, no one could deny the fact that faith-based organizations have a proven track record of helping others. All across the nation, on any given day, selfless followers of Jesus give of their time and material substance to share God's message of love and hope. They communicate through words and music in worship services held in missions, jails, nursing homes, hospitals, and care centers, but they also serve meals, read to the visually impaired, drive elderly patients to their doctors' offices, share quiet moments with the grieving, pass out sandwiches and coffee to the homeless, deliver groceries and clothing to needy families, help victims of tornadoes or floods rebuild their homes and their lives, and offer their services in many other ways. These are the kind of unsung heroes President George Bush, Sr. called "a thousand points of light." They are unselfish 21st -century disciples engaged in fulfilling Jesus' command to "let your light shine before men, that they may see your good deeds and praise your Father in heaven."

In pre-electricity days, a lamplighter making his rounds at dusk and igniting one street lamp after another, was asked by a young boy, "Sir, what are you doing?"

"I am poking holes in the darkness," the lamplighter answered.

Followers of Jesus can poke huge holes in the moral and spiritual darkness that is blanketing our nation. By rejecting the rule of materialism and accepting the rule of Jesus, we can serve others selflessly in His name and shine the glory of God across America.

For Personal Reflection and/or Group Discussion

1. What attitudes should a believer hold about material possessions?

2. Why do you agree or disagree that a believer is wise to have a retirement plan?

3. How can a wealthy person live by faith?

4. How can a low-income person be materialistic?

5. What would you say if you were asked, "What's so great about rewards in heaven?"

6. Why is material prosperity alone not a true measure of a nation's greatness?

7. What might convince unbelieving neighbors that owning a home in heaven is more important than owning a home on earth?

8. How would you teach your children to be grateful to the Lord for home, food, clothes, and possessions?

9. How can you teach them the value of serving others?

10. What top three tips would you give if an engaged couple asked you for financial counsel?

Chapter 4

THE "RELIGIOUS" SINS

Fascinated by a penny weight scale in an antique store, Sam stepped onto it and dropped a penny into the coin slot. Out popped a fortune-and-weight card. He began reading it to his wife: "You are an intelligent, handsome person. You will obtain great wealth and . . . "

Snatching the card from Sam, his wife announced, "Look, Sam. It has your weight wrong too."

Human nature tends to make us prone to *the subtle sin of deception.* History records instances of deception even among America's elected officials. Although the majority of our elected public servants have had a sterling track record, some have dirtied the track. Congressman Condit, for example, sullied his reputation by deceiving the D.C. police about his affair with Chandra Levy. He later admitted he had not told the truth, but the prior deception seriously damaged his reputation. President Bill Clinton deceived the nation when he denied any sexual involvement with Monica Lewinsky. President Nixon practiced deception in the Watergate Scandal. President Warren G. Harding's secretary of the interior, Senator Albert B. Fall, practiced deception by secretly leasing naval oil reserve lands to private companies. In return, he received about $400,000 in gifts and loans from several oilmen. When the *slick* deal was exposed as the Teapot Dome Scandal, Fall was fined $100,000 and sentenced to one year in prison.

Not long ago, six people made payments of more than $1 million to a man who claimed to operate an aircraft sales business over the Internet. He told the buyers that he would deliver eight planes and four airplane engines. However, he didn't own the planes or the engines. Inevitably, a federal grand jury grounded this "high-flying" deceiver; it indicted him on eight counts of wire fraud. Each criminal count comes with a $250,000 fine and a five-year prison sentence.

Not all deception is as notorious as the Teapot Dome Scandal or the Internet wire fraud, but all deceptive practices offend God. We may deceive ourselves into thinking we are smarter, better looking, and more talented than we actually are. Or we may deceive others by telling lies or half-truths. "You look absolutely stunning," may be an insult disguised as a compliment.

Deception extends even to religion. Smooth-talking religious charlatans have deceived followers into almost everything from giving them large sums of money to committing mass suicide. Jesus called their kind "false prophets" and "wolves in sheep's clothing." The apostle John commented that "many deceivers . . . have gone out into the world" (2 John 7). A recent news article reported that from 1999 to 2001 securities regulators in 27 states pursued legal action against companies and individuals that used spiritual or religious beliefs to prey on more than 90,000 investors and scam them out of billions of dollars. The article alleges that about 20,000 investors were duped into mortgaging their homes, accumulating huge credit card bills or cashing in their retirement funds on the promise of enormous gains from investments in precious metals mines and cargo ships.

But religious people may dupe themselves as well as be duped. Even church members may be guilty of the subtle sin of deception. Some have settled into a rut (sometimes defined as a grave with the ends kicked out) but try to appear "spiritual." Their souls have become as dry as an Arizona desert and their commitment to Jesus Christ as shaky as gelatin. They attend church services but merely mouth religious words, exchange religious greetings, and drop a token donation into the offering plate. They are like the tightwad who sang to himself every time he contributed a dollar: "When we asunder part, it gives me inward pain." Some others practiced deception by pretending to have faith in Jesus Christ in order to gain membership. Their motive in joining may have been a desire for more business contacts or respectability or social opportunities.

According to a humorous, but insightful story, a group of male teens plotted to disrupt a meeting of a congregation known for its extremely emotional worship. The teens outfitted one of their number with a red devil's costume, complete with horns, a pointed tail, and a pitchfork, and hid in some shrubs outside the church. When they heard the worship inside reach a fever pitch, they opened the church's entrance door and pushed "the devil" inside. Seeing "the devil" approaching them, the congregants rushed for the back and side doors. However, one gentleman tripped on torn carpet in the center aisle and fell head over heels. He alone was left to face "the devil." Visibly shaken and looking up from the floor, he urged: "Stay right where you are, Mr. Devil. I have been a member of this church for thirty-seven years—but I've been on your side the whole time."

Judas Iscariot, one of Jesus' 12 disciples, was particularly adept at practicing deception. Like the other 11, he followed Jesus throughout Palestine, listened to His words, pledged his allegiance to Jesus, and shared mealtimes with Him. Yet, Judas was a deceiver. Although he did not fool Jesus, this crafty disciple-treasurer feigned devotion to Jesus by greeting Him with a kiss. The kiss served as a signal to armed guards that Jesus was the man they wanted to arrest. The deception was rooted in Judas's love of money. He betrayed Jesus for 30 pieces of silver (Matthew 27:3, 4).

A love of money often leads to the subtle sin of deception. A salesman may pad his expense account and rationalize this deceptive practice by reminding himself that he hasn't had a raise in more than two years. A married couple may falsify their income tax returns in order to reduce what they owe the state or federal government. *Taxes are far too high, and the government wastes our tax dollars,* they reason. A husband may deceive his wife by secretly withdrawing funds from his 401K, an account he had promised to keep intact for their retirement years. A wife may deceive her husband by purchasing Powerball tickets whenever she buys gas at a local convenience store. She knows they agreed not to gamble, but she reasons, "His attitude will change big time when I win the jackpot."

The Book of Acts shows how a love of money and the subtle sin of deception were linked in the attitude and behavior of Ananias and Sapphira, a married couple in the church at Jerusalem. The church at that time teemed with converts from many countries. They had come to Jerusalem to participate in Jewish festivals. While there, they heard the apostle Peter preach about Jesus, the Messiah, who had been crucified and entombed, but arose from the dead and was seen by many of His followers. They believed Peter's message, repented, decided to follow Jesus, and settled down in Jerusalem—without the means to support themselves. That's when the rest of the congregation pitched in to help. They shared their possessions with those in need. Those who owned real estate, sold it, and gave it to the apostles to distribute to the needy. Barnabas, who later engaged in disciple-making outside

Palestine, is cited in Acts 4:36 and 37 as one who sold land and donated the proceeds to the church's relief program. Ananias and Sapphira also participated in the relief program, but in a bizarre way.

Acts 5:1 and 2 reports what they did. They sold a piece of property, but agreed to give only part of the proceeds to the church's relief program. The rest would line Ananias's pockets. Of course, the church had not demanded any amount of money from them or anyone else. However, Ananias gave the apostles the impression that the donation represented the full amount of the sale. When the apostle Peter confronted Ananias about his subtle sin of deception, Ananias experienced immediate divine judgment. He fell down dead (see verses 3-5). Three hours later (perhaps she had gone shopping), Sapphira entered the place where the apostles and other disciples were gathered. When she assured Peter that Ananias had donated the full amount of the real estate proceeds, Peter exposed her sin of deception and announced that she would share the same fate that had struck her husband. Instantly, she collapsed stone dead (see verses 7-10).

These were highly unusual circumstances. If what happened to Ananias and Sapphira were to happen today to everyone who practices deception, our planet would realize zero population. So why did God judge Ananias and Sapphira so dramatically? Because the event occurred at the beginning of the church's history, it seems that God was sending a message not only to the congregation in Jerusalem but to all future congregations—He demands integrity on the part of all who follow His Son.

The subtle sin of self-righteousness is another "religious" sin. Many Americans expect to go to Heaven when they die, because they believe their good deeds outweigh their bad deeds and therefore tip the judgment scales in their favor. However, the Bible explains that passports to Heaven are granted only to those whose faith rests in Jesus, not in their own good works. Jesus declared, "I am the way and the truth and the life. No one comes to the Father except through me" (John 14:6). Ephesians 2:8-10 affirms Jesus' declaration: "For it is by grace you have been saved, through faith—and this not from yourselves, it is the gift of God—not by works, so that no one can boast. For we are God's workmanship, created in Christ Jesus to do good works, which God prepared in advance for us to do." Clearly, faith in Christ should be followed by good works, but good works cannot substitute for faith in Christ!

Also, those who rely on regular church attendance to get them to heaven are only deceiving themselves. Entrance into heaven does not depend upon having one's name in a church attendance book but in the book of life (see Revelation 20:11-15).

Hypocrisy is another subtle "religious" sin. Who hasn't heard someone say. "I don't attend church because the church is full of hypocrites"? God doesn't ban hypocrites from church. If they are present, at least they have an opportunity to hear something that will challenge them to abandon their hypocrisy. They can learn and heed the fact that God's "worshipers must worship in spirit and in truth" (John 4:24).

Of course, hypocrisy isn't unique to the 21st century. Speaking to the nation of Judah through the prophet Isaiah around 700 B.C., the Lord indicted the people for their hypocrisy. While offering sacrifices to the Lord and observing religious festivals, their hearts were far from Him. They put on a good show of religion, but their social injustices and personal immorality caused the Lord to hide His eyes from them and reject their prayers. He summoned the nation to repent and receive His cleansing and forgiveness (see Isaiah 1:10-18).

In His encounters with the teachers of the law and the Pharisees, first-century Jewish religious leaders, Jesus often impugned their hypocrisy. He said they observed the external details of their religion but were "full of greed and self-indulgence (Matthew 23:25). He said they looked beautiful on the outside in their religious garb and appeared righteous but were full of hypocrisy and wickedness on the inside (verses 27, 28). They loved to pray long prayers in public places to appear righteous, but they didn't fool God (Matthew 6:5).

The Bruised Pharisees were particularly hypocritical. They taught that a man must not cast a lingering look at a woman. So when a woman approached any of them, they purposely turned their heads and walked into a tree in a show of religiosity. Hence, the name "Bruised Pharisees."

Bruised Pharisees are no longer on the planet, but hypocrisy remains in spite of the Biblical command to rid ourselves of it (1 Peter 2:1). Knowing that the word "hypocrite" comes from a Greek word signifying *to act behind a mask,* we can see how it relates to play-acting one's devotion to God. Even the most spiritual-sounding prayers can be hypocritical.

A story relates that a pastor and a deacon purchased parrots that were guaranteed to talk. But what they would say was not guaranteed. It turned out that the deacon's parrot would say only, "Let's pray. Let's pray," whereas the pastor's parrot would say only, "Let's kiss. Let's kiss."

Concerned that church members visiting his home would hear "Let's kiss. Let's kiss," the pastor played tapes he hoped would persuade his parrot to change and increase its vocabulary. But nothing worked. The parrot seemed undaunted in its determination to say only, "Let's kiss. Let's kiss."

To make matters worse, the deacon jokingly chided the pastor. "Look," he said, "I'm only a deacon, but you're a pastor. Yet, my parrot is more spiritual than yours. My parrot says, 'Let's pray. Let's pray.' Yours will only say, 'Let's kiss. Let's kiss.'"

Exasperated, the pastor begged the deacon to consent to getting the two parrots together. He hoped the deacon's parrot's spirituality might rub off on his worldly parrot.

The deacon agreed.

When the two parrots were side by side in the pastor's home, the men stepped outside the room and listened for some parrot talk. Sure enough, the pastor's parrot spoke up. "Let's kiss. Let's kiss," it squawked.

Then, to their astonishment, the deacon's parrot exclaimed, "At last my prayers have been answered!"

We have all brushed up against *the subtle sin of condescension,* or perhaps been guilty of it ourselves. It's the holier-than-thou attitude than conveys the impression that it is truly humbling to acknowledge the existence of someone less holy. It is a "religious" sin that conveys the attitude, "Touch me and receive merit," or "You are so fortunate to make my acquaintance," or "I am a very important person, but I will try to spare a moment of my time for you." This subtle sin, like all the rest, erects a roadblock in the way of discipling others. It leads some people to say, "If that's the way Jesus' followers are, I don't want to be one of them."

Even those who endeavor to disciple the homeless, the indigent, the addicted, and the lonely can be guilty of the subtle sin of condescension. Case in point: A group from a fashionable suburban church conducts a worship service once a month at a rescue mission. They enter through a private rear door, have coffee and pastries in a private room, then pass through another private door and onto the platform just in time for the worship service to begin. Their expensive suits and dresses form quite a contrast to the worn, soiled clothes worn by the rescue mission crowd. The group leader announces that he and his friends are happy to be at the mission to talk and sing about Jesus. Forty-five minutes later, the group exits the platform through the private back door, enjoy a few more refreshments in the private room, then leave the building and drive home.

Put yourself in the shoes of any needy person in the rescue mission audience—at least for a moment. How would you feel if you heard the group leader say how pleased he and his group were to be there and to talk about Jesus? How would feel about the group's platform entrance and exit through a private back door? How would you feel when you heard about Jesus' all-embracing love from a group of disciples who failed to show you any love—not even a handshake or a listening ear. You might be able to name the subtle sin of condescension, but you know you witnessed it.

Contrast the foregoing scenes with those of a different group of disciples. They, too, have come from a suburban church to minister to men and women at the rescue mission. They are wearing casual clothes. Before the service begins, they mingle with the audience and discover they have much in common. Each group member meets someone from the same home town, someone else who used to be in the same line of work, someone else whose kids back home are the same ages as the group member's, and someone else who is a fellow alumnus of his or her *alma mater*. The group members also have opportunity to encourage those men and women, telling them about Jesus' love and His power to make a difference. Then they step onto the platform and conduct the service; and before leaving, they mingle once again with the audience.

Again, put yourself in the shoes of any needy person in the rescue mission audience—at least for a moment. How do you feel now? You have experienced Jesus' love channeled through His humble disciples. You did not witness the sin of condescension this time, and you are eager to trust in Jesus for salvation and the power to transform your life.

Wood carvers fascinate those who watch them take a block of wood and turn it into a lifelike carving of a horse or a bear or a dog or an eagle or some other animal or object. How do they do it? Extraordinary talent plays a role, but so does imaging. If a wood craftsman sets out to carve a mustang, he keeps the image of that kind of horse in his mind's eye. Then he chips away everything that isn't "mustang" until only a mustang remains.

Like a master craftsman, God chips away from our lives everything that isn't Christlike. Ultimately, His work on us will end. When we reach heaven, we will be like Christ. No sinful blemishes, bumps, rough spots, or ragged edges will remain. Between now and then, though, we need to cooperate with God. We need to conduct daily self-examination, confess our sins—even our subtle "religious" sins, and forsake everything that contrasts with Jesus' character.

Our nation needs an unobstructed view of Jesus, the King of kings and Lord of lords.

For Personal Reflection and/or Group Discussion

1. What political deception have you witnessed in your generation?

2. What religious deception have you witnessed in your generation?

3. Why is it foolish to try to deceive God?

4. What masks might a hypocrite hide behind at church?

5. How can a follower of Jesus strip hypocrisy from his or her life?

6. How did Jesus' life and ministry show that He correctly identified Himself as "the truth" (John 14:6)?

7. How do you feel when you are the victim of a condescending attitude?

8. Why is it futile for someone to think he or she is good enough to be admitted into heaven?

9. How might you demonstrate to your neighbors that your faith in Jesus is real?

10. How can you share Jesus' love with a homeless person without having a condescending attitude?

Chapter 5

GREEN EYES MAY BE PRETTY, BUT NOT THESE GREEN EYES

What color are your eyes? If they are green, you aren't exactly in the world's largest eye-color group. You have probably noticed that brown and blue eyes far outnumber green. But green eyes are pretty, especially in combination with a beautiful smile.

Of course, there is a down side to green eyes. Jealousy is often called the green-eyed monster, and jealousy is anything but attractive. Galatians 5:20 associates jealousy with idolatry and witchcraft, and Proverbs 14:30 equates jealousy's alter ego, envy, with a rotting of the bones. You might say jealousy and envy are as ugly as sin! And you would be right, because both are sins—subtle sins.

The subtle sin of jealousy is aimed at those whom we perceive to be rivals; whereas *the subtle sin of envy* is aimed at what our rivals have that we want. For example, Bella has fallen in love with Cory, a college classmate. The two have dated several times, but Cory hasn't even hinted at a serious relationship. The other day, Bella saw Cory and a sorority sister, Twila, sitting together in the Student Union Building. She flew into a rage, walked over to the two, and blurted out, "Twila, I thought you were my friend, but you're nothing but a scummy low life. I can't believe you would flirt with my boyfriend behind my back. I'll never speak to you again!" Spinning around on her heels, Bella stormed out of the building.

The next afternoon, Bella was working at her part-time sales clerk job at a boutique when her Science lab partner, Melanie, showed up. "Hi, Bella," she began, "what do you have in a silk scarf that would look really hot on me when I drive around in my BRAND-NEW MERCEDES CONVERTIBLE? Did you know about the car? My parents surprised me with it yesterday."

Bella was already envious of Melanie's circumstances, knowing that Melanie's parents were funding her education and keeping her supplied with credit cards. Now they had given her a Mercedes!

Envy swelled up inside Bella. Her face turned red, and her shoulders drooped. "That's nice," she said matter-of-factly. "The scarves are on Aisle 5 on the left."

The subtle sins of jealousy and envy had struck like vipers into Bella's soul, spewing venom into her thoughts, attitudes, and actions. She became unhappy, curt, quarrelsome, and aloof. Her grades slipped, her relationships soured, and her work at the boutique slumped. However, one day Bella came across something that radically changed her outlook on life. While browsing through a bookstore in the mall, she saw a little book of meditations. Intrigued, she picked it up and opened it at random to a page titled, "In the Grip of Twin Monsters." As she read, she understood that the "monsters" were *the subtle sins, Jealousy and Envy*. The meditation quoted Galatians 5:19-21, a passage of Scripture that puts jealousy and envy in the same category as sexual immorality, impurity, debauchery, idolatry, witchcraft, drunkenness, and orgies. She had always assumed that she was moral and upright, but now she faced the reality that her jealousy and envy were as offensive to God as some sins she would never think of committing. The meditation also prescribed confessing jealousy and envy to God and to the offended parties. Bella knew she needed to have a talk with God, but also with Cory, Twila, and Melanie. Peace was already seeping into her mind and heart.

History's first account of jealousy and envy appears in Genesis, chapter 4. They served as motives for the first murder. Adam and Eve's son Cain murdered his younger brother Abel.

Here's what led to the heinous crime. Cain, a farmer, brought some of his produce to the Lord as an offering (Genesis 4:3). Abel, a shepherd, brought fat portions from some of the firstborn of his flock (verse 4). The Lord accepted Abel's offering but rejected Cain's. Feeling the pain of having his offering rejected by the Lord, Cain's jealousy and envy churned and boiled over in a rage. He was jealous of his brother, envious of his acceptance by the Lord, and angry enough to plot his death. Although the Lord gave Cain a second opportunity to worship Him correctly, Cain rejected it. Next, he invited Abel to walk into a field with him, where he assaulted and killed him (verse 8).

The familiar Bible story about Joseph and his coat of many colors zeroes in on another case of sibling rivalry fueled by jealousy. Joseph's ten older brothers despised him, because he blabbed to Daddy about their poor work habits. Also, they despised Joseph because their father Jacob had given him a multicolored coat, an obvious sign of his special love for him. They hated Joseph so much that they would not speak even one kind word to him. The fuse on the powder keg burned dangerously low when Joseph told them his dreams. The first involved his brothers' sheaves of wheat bowing down to his upright sheaf. The second dream featured the sun, moon, and 11 stars bowing down to Joseph. The moon and star represented Joseph's parents; the 11 stars, Joseph's ten older brothers and his younger brother. The jealous brothers got the picture! Joseph was saying he would reign over them. Genesis 37:11 reports they were jealous of him. According to verses 19, 20, they conspired to kill him. However, Reuben, the oldest brother talked them out of the scheme. At his suggestion, the brothers threw Joseph into a pit and later, when Reuben was absent, sold Joseph to some Midianites who were journeying to Egypt. They, in turn, sold Joseph to Potiphar, an Egyptian official.

Having rid themselves of Joseph, the brothers hatched an evil coverup. They smeared Joseph's coat with goat blood, carried it home to their father, and reported that a wild animal had killed Joseph. Their jealousy had led them down a trail of murderous thoughts, treachery, and deceit.

A few centuries later, jealousy drove Israel's King Saul to attempt murder. His target was David, who would later become Israel's king. At first, Saul liked David. After all, David had stepped up to the plate and killed the Philistine giant Goliath, thereby saving the day for Israel. Also, David's soothing harp music had calmed Saul's frazzled nerves on a number of occasions. But Saul's attitude toward David turned vicious when he heard the women of Israel praise David's military accomplishments to the tune of "Saul has slain his thousands, and David his tens of thousands" (1 Samuel 18:7). Saul reasoned that David's skyrocketing popularity would catapult him to the throne. Verse 8 opens the door to Saul's thoughts and feelings at the time. "Saul was very angry; this refrain galled him. 'They have credited David with tens of thousands,' he thought, 'but me with only thousands. What more can he get but the kingdom?'" Verse 9 adds: "And from that time on Saul kept a jealous eye on David."

We can well imagine that Saul tossed and turned in his royal bed that night as jealousy churned in his soul. The next day, when David was playing the harp, Saul hurled a spear and David, hoping to run it through him and pin him to the wall. He missed, and tried again. Another miss! Recognizing that the Lord was on David's side, Saul transferred David from music duty to active military duty. Before long, though, David had to flee from Saul and hide as a fugitive. But the day arrived when Saul's career ended in death at the hands of the Philistines and David succeeded him to the throne.

Jesus, David's preeminent descendant, was also the target of anger based in jealousy and envy. These twin monsters followed Him all the way to the Cross. Pontius Pilate, the Roman governor of Judea at the time, knew Jesus was innocent of the charges brought against Him by the Jews' corrupt religious leaders. Matthew 27:18 reports that "he knew it was out of envy that they had handed Jesus over to him." Nevertheless, Pilate attached a higher value to his political career than to justice. Wanting to avert a riot that would make him look bad in the eyes of the Roman emperor, he let an angry mob decide Jesus' fate. Led on by the envious religious leaders, the rabble rousers screamed, "Crucify him. Crucify him!" (verses 22, 23). Then Pilate washed his hands—as if he could wash away his guilt—and had Jesus flogged before handing Him over for crucifixion (verse 26).

Why were the corrupt Jewish leaders envious of Jesus? They resented His power and popularity. He had captured the admiration of great numbers of people by teaching with authority and significance, by healing the sick and befriending the friendless. Matthew 7:28 and 29 paints a striking contrast between His teaching and the religious leaders' teaching: " . . . the crowds were amazed at his [Jesus'] teaching, because he taught as one who had authority, and not as their teachers of the law." Mark 12:37 reports that when Jesus answered a religious teacher's question, "the large crowd listened to him with delight."

Jealousy and envy still lurk in the human heart and afflict injury and pain. A jealous estranged husband fires a bullet into the skull of his wife's boyfriend. A thief sneaks into a house to steal from others what he wants for himself. A shunned teenager, envious of the attention paid to the football players at his high school, carries a concealed gun to class, and uses it to assassinate several of them. A jealous employee, fearing his rival will receive the available managerial position, spreads malicious lies about him. A mother, jealous of her newly married son's devotion to his wife, badmouths her constantly.

The subtle sins of jealousy and envy can erupt even among people who are supposed to be on the same side. Two pastors in the same denomination became jealous of each other and stopped speaking to each other. Years passed and erased their memory of the cause of their mutual jealousy, but they still disliked and avoided each other. Eventually, though, something unlikely occurred that turned these two foes into friends.

The men registered a couple of hours apart for a large interdenominational conference in a major Canadian city. Each received the address of a private residence where he would be staying free of charge during the conference. The first man arrived that night at the assigned address and was escorted to a guest bedroom having a double bed. To his utter astonishment, 15 minutes later his old nemesis appeared. He had been assigned the same address and bedroom. The two glared at each other, then eyed the double bed. Each noticed that it sagged in the middle. Finally, one said to the other, "If you and I are going to sleep in *that* bed, we had better forgive each other and ask the Lord to forgive us too." Both laughed, prayed, and enjoyed a reasonably good night's sleep.

No one has to be convinced that jealousy and envy are far from extinct, but who would suspect that *the subtle sin of idolatry* is also far from extinct, even woven into the fabric of contemporary life? To be sure, some our contemporaries worship idols—little gods made by human hands—and pray to them daily—but idols come in a variety of forms. Objects of worship include oneself, money, cars, houses, entertainment celebrities, superstar athletes, popularity, success, fame, education, the environment, and even one's own children.

In the first century, the apostle Paul challenged idolatry wherever he traveled in the Roman Empire. He engaged in discipleship in cities where idolatry ranged from Emperor worship to the worship of the stars and planets. The pagan population in Ephesus worshiped Diana, the love goddess. Aphrodite captured the Corinthians' worship. One thousand prostitutes plied their wicked trade at the temple of Aphrodite. In the city of Colosse, the worship of angels and other spirits was commonplace. At Athens, statues erected to honor pagan deities dotted the city. However, many pagans became Jesus' followers due to the faithful discipling efforts of Paul and other believers. Like the brand-new Thessalonian disciples, they "turned to God from idols to serve the living and true God" (1 Thessalonians 1:9).

Most of us are too sophisticated to worship idols carved from wood or stone, and few of us trust what we read in astrology columns. Nevertheless, *the subtle sin of idolatry* grips us if we value anything or anyone more than the true and living God. The apostle Paul went so far as to accuse some misguided individuals of worshiping food. He wrote that their god was their stomach (Philippians 3:19). Likely, a bloated god! Perhaps Paul's words should give us pause for thought the next time we sit down to an all-you-can-eat buffet.

With Israel and the Middle East gaining so much attention in the news, books about end-time events are almost jumping from store shelves into the hands of millions of consumers. Readers want to know about the Rapture, Jesus' Second Coming, Armageddon, and the Antichrist. Although writers of books on end-time events occasionally resort to conjecture (for example, the Bible does not specifically name any individual "Antichrist"), we know absolutely that idolatry will flourish in the end-time. Revelation 13 predicts it. A false prophet will construct an animated image of an extremely powerful and wicked political figure in the rebuilt Jewish temple in Jerusalem. Those who refuse to worship this idol will be sentenced to death.

In spite of the death threat, though, a remnant of faithful followers of Jesus will not cave in to the order to worship the idol. Just as Daniel's three friends defied the edict to worship King Nebuchadnezzar's image (see Daniel 3), so these end-time believers will shun idolatry and lock their fate in God's hands. And, just as God delivered Daniel's friends from death, so God will keep many alive who refuse to bow down to the image constructed in honor of the most wicked political figure in history. When God drops the curtain on the career of the false prophet and his diabolical political crony, He will punish them and their followers. They will be out of business permanently, but Jesus' followers will emerge victorious and joyful. They will stand with Jesus, the Lamb, on Mount Zion, and sing a new song celebrating their deliverance. Earth's malicious reign of terror is behind them and Jesus' magnificent reign of peace and righteousness awaits them (see Revelation 14:1-5).

The human race seems to have a built-in need and capacity to worship, but so many men and women have substituted false gods for the true God. Those who follow Jesus must evaluate their lives, put aside the subtle sin of idolatry, and dedicate themselves to the great work of discipling our nation in this generation. The United States can experience the blessings of being truly "one nation under God."

"Dear children, keep yourselves from idols" (1 John 5:21).

For Personal Reflection and/or Group Discussion

1. What crimes have you read about or heard about that were committed because of jealousy?

2. What would you tell a friend who said he or she envied your job?

3. What made you aware of jealousy for the first time in your life?

4. What distinction(s) do you make between jealousy and envy?

5. How would you feel if a fellow employee received the promotion you wanted and felt you deserved? How could God help you deal with negative thoughts and emotions?

6. What would it say about your devotion to the Lord if you sincerely congratulated the person who was promoted?

7. How can parents cope successfully with sibling rivalry on the part of their children?

8. How common is idolatry in the United States? Explain.

9. How do some parents show that they worship their children?

10. How can followers of Jesus show in simple ways that they truly love God?

11. What connection do you see between the devil's evil activities today and his envy of Jesus?

12. How might credit card spending become a tool in the hands of the subtle sin of envy?

Chapter 6

ANGER AND OTHER COMBUSTIBLE EMOTIONS

The Reforma section of Guadalajara, Mexico's second largest city, resembled a bombed-out area in 1992 after at least nine explosions tore through the earth for a mile, creating large holes and huge craters of 50 meters in diameter. Numerous vehicles, including a bus were gobbled up by the craters. The explosions killed 200 people and injured 600. More than 1,000 buildings in 20 blocks were damaged by the blasts. Fire Chief Jose Trinidad Lopez Rivas was said to have surmised that thousands of liters of gasoline in the sewer system triggered the explosions. PEMEX, the Mexican state petroleum company blamed the explosions on a leak of the extremely flammable chemical Hexane from a local factory.

Explosions similar to the one in Mexico have occurred at other times and in other countries, but they are infrequent compared with volatile eruptions of anger and other combustive emotions. Anger, hatred, hostility, resentment, and a spirit of rebellion explode with deadly force daily in every community. Perhaps not a minute passes without an outburst of at least one of these hazardous emotions.

Hatred, resentment, anger, hostility and a spirit of rebellion unleash themselves in such situations as workplace disputes, marital spats, neighborhood disagreements, political strife, and wars. Remember when "postal" referred to the mail and "ballistic" described a missile? Now "postal" and "ballistic" commonly refer to anger and hostility that have blown the lid off civility and boiled over in aggressive actions.

Recently, a mob in Mexico City beat a 29-year-old man to death and tied his body to a gazebo in front of a police station. Why such extreme anger? The victim was suspected of stealing a statue of the neighborhood's patron saint. Some angry residents had even rung their church's bell to rally people to participate in the beating.

Also, not long ago, a Bible quoting competition in a southern U.S. city ended in the murder of one of the two finalists. After the two had argued over the wording of a verse of Scripture, one rushed home, picked up a gun, returned, and shot the other.

Church history records thousands of Christian martyrdoms at the hands of angry members of other religions. Today, too, persecution and martyrdom face many followers of Jesus in countries hostile to Christianity.

Of course, Christians themselves can get angry and step over the line and into aggressive behavior. But most often we harbor *anger, hatred, hostility, resentment, and a spirit of rebellion as subtle sins.* They choke our joy, rob us of peace, smother our love, and disrupt our fellowship with God, but we cater to them as much as a doting parent caters to the whims of a spoiled child.

Churches never split over love. They split because one faction resents another. The issue might be worship style, building program, youth ministry, the minister's family, allocation of funds, or something else, but anger and hostility run amok. In some situations the anger gets so hot it almost steams the stained glass windows.

One church in a "snowbird" state found itself torn apart by angry factions. The 65-and-older members of the congregation were perceived by the younger members as resisting change and impeding the church's progress. The 65-and-older members accused the younger group of shunning them and even treating them with disdain. Instead of trying to repair the rip, the minister only made it worse by siding with the younger members. One fateful Sunday morning he remarked from the pulpit that he would be pleased to see the seniors' caskets lined up in front of the platform. Further, he remarked that he would preach their funeral sermon and never shed a tear.

It was the seniors' last Sunday in that church. The following Sunday they worshiped in a rented school auditorium. The local newspaper later published the story of the hostile church split. The caption under a photo of the new "old" congregation announced: "Senior citizens worship in exile."

What could have been a beautiful picture of forgiveness, love, mutual consideration, compromise, and reconciliation had become an ugly representation of anger, hatred, resentment, and hostility. The community was left to wonder why those who professed to follow Jesus could divide and take opposite paths.

The subtle sins of anger and resentment can inflict emotional and physical harm on oneself as well as on those against whom they are directed. They may contribute to such abnormalities as irritability, negative thinking, antisocial behavior, high blood pressure, headaches, indigestion, and insomnia. A person filled with anger and resentment expends time and energy nursing his or her hurt and thinking negatively about the person or persons who caused the hurt. By dwelling on the hurt the offended person actually increases the damage done by the offender.

Joseph, the slave who became a savior to the Egyptians by following a divinely inspired famine-survival plan, could have been angry with his brothers and resented their malicious act of selling him into slavery. He could have been angry with God, too, for letting a series of tragic events happen to him. But Joseph understood that God controls even negative circumstances for the positive good of His people. So, when Joseph reconciled with his brothers, he told them, "Don't be afraid. Am I in the place of God? You intended to harm me, but God intended it for good to accomplish what is now being done, the saving of many lives" (Genesis 50:19, 20).

About 1,500 years later, Jesus was nailed to the Cross. Instead of spewing anger and resentment upon those who crucified Him, He prayed, "Father, forgive them, for they do not know what they are doing" (Luke 23:34).

A baseball game and a pleasant afternoon go together like cotton candy and a kid. The fans sit back and enjoy America's greatest pastime. What is so tranquil as an inning of pitches, hits, and runs—that is, if your team is winning and the umpire calls things your way? But can you picture the bench-clearing brawls that would occur if there were no umpire? Whether we agree with an umpire or not, we recognize that he is a necessary peace-keeping force. By comparison, Christ's peace acts as an umpire in Christian relationships. Instead of being angry with others in the congregation and resenting real or imagined offenses against us, we are supposed to "let the peace of Christ rule [umpire] in your hearts, since as members of one body you were called to peace" (Colossians 3:15). Without regard for Christ's peace, we might not have a pew-clearing brawl but we will surely have hard feelings, bickering, and division.

To be fair, it must be said that not all anger is sinful. We learn from John, chapter 2, that Jesus expressed anger, but it was righteous anger. He was angry with those who had turned the temple, a house of prayer, into a house of commerce. Merchants had set up shop in the temple's outer court, selling sacrificial animals to those who had traveled far to observe the Passover. Moneychangers were on hand to exchange the worshipers' coins into currency that would be accepted for the annual temple tax and certain offerings. Abhorring this disregard for His Father's house as a holy place of worship, Jesus made a whip of palm branches and used it to rout the moneychangers, the merchants, and their animals from the temple. He also scattered the moneychangers' coins and overturned their tables (see John 2:12-16).

Clearly, Jesus was angered by actions that offended God, and as God's sinless Son, He had the right to execute judgment on the guilty. We may be angry with actions that offend God, but we do not have the right to take matters into our own hands. The justice system can punish lawbreakers, and ultimately God will judge all who violate His moral law. Romans 12:19 counsels: "Do not take revenge, my friends, but leave room for God's wrath, for it is written, 'it is mine to avenge; I will repay,' says the Lord."

But knowing God will punish wrongdoers does not exempt us from taking appropriate action to combat the onslaught of the immorality and irreverence. We must not sit back, fold our hands, close our eyes, and sigh, "Who are we to judge? We can't force society to change the situation, and after all, someday God will punish wrongdoing and make everything right." Nor should we succumb to the temptation to lower our standards to the level of those who offend God. Those who do so may salve their consciences by insisting this is the twenty-first century and they don't want to be considered old-fashioned or obscurantist.

Didn't the apostle Paul stir his Christian readers to show righteous indignation over the evil present in their society? He encouraged them to "have nothing to do with the fruitless deeds of darkness, but rather expose them" (Ephesians 5:11). He challenged them to "be very careful, then, how you live—not as unwise but as wise, making the most of every opportunity, because the days are evil" (verses 15, 16).

You have visited a restaurant with dim lighting, haven't you? You followed the host or hostess down a dark aisle to a table, where you sat and strained your eyes to read the menu. (Perhaps the darkness is intentionally planned to keep customers from seeing the high prices listed in small print.) But something strange happened after you ordered your food; your eyes gradually adjusted to the darkness. By the time you left the restaurant the darkness didn't bother you at all.

Have we Christians been immersed in a dark culture for such a long time that we have grown accustomed to the darkness? Recalling a recent "Christian" social event may help you decide. Did off-color jokes slip into the conversation? How often did you hear the name "God" used as a thoughtless exclamation? Did blatantly immoral movies or TV shows become topics of favorable mention? What, if anything, made the occasion different from a nonChristian social gathering?

Christian pollsters report an alarming similarity between secular and Christian lifestyles, shrinking confidence in the Bible as absolute truth, and a fading commitment to Christ. Apparently, we who profess to follow Jesus are swerving from the straight and narrow way. Instead of setting our sights on the Celestial City, we have fixed a longing gaze on Vanity Fair. We seem to be more interested in fun than faith. Happiness has replaced holiness as an essential goal of Christian living. Rampant wickedness in our culture should anger us, not attract us. We should invade the darkness, not invite it into our lives. We should break our alliance with the darkness, confess our waywardness to Jesus, the Light of the World, and commit ourselves anew to the task of discipling men and women who are victims of the darkness?

Righteous anger should be directed at sin, not sinners. It is right to feel angry about child abuse, murder, drug traffic, pornography, homosexuality, abortion, embezzlement, scams, gang activity, and a host of other outbreaks of violence and shameful behavior. It is not right to bomb an abortion clinic, threaten the lives of doctors who perform abortions, or lynch child abusers, drug pushers, pornography dealers, gays, swindlers, embezzlers, scam artists, and gang bangers. *Hatred and hostility are subtle sins* that are devilish, dangerous, and disgusting. Instead of harboring hatred and showing hostility, Jesus' modern disciples must follow His example of love. When accused of eating with tax collectors (considered swindlers and disloyal to the Jews) and sinners, Jesus explained, "It is not the healthy who need a doctor, but the sick. . . . I have not come to call the righteous, but sinners" (Matthew 9:12, 13). Like Jesus, who displayed the most extraordinary love by dying on the cross for sinners—including you and me—

we ought to love even those whose lifestyles offend God and us. After all, divine love can transform even the most vile sinner into a forgiven and committed follower of Jesus. It happened to Saul of Tarsus, who described himself as "the worst of sinners" (1 Timothy 1:16). After believing in Jesus, Saul became known as the apostle Paul, indisputably the greatest discipler of all time.

Rebellion lies at the root of sin. Abusers, drug dealers, pornographers, murderers, swindlers, gays, and others who offend our sensibilities are rebels. They fly in the face of decency and civility. They defy either the law of the land or the law of God or in most cases both. We can read rebellion in the facial expression of the criminal who grins from the back of a police car or from the front of a courtroom. We see it in the outlandish dress and mannerisms displayed in a gay pride parade. We view it in tattoos and body piercing—pierced eyebrows, pierced noses, pierced navels, and even pierced tongues—and we hear it in rap and hip-hop music. We encounter it in news reports of coups, terrorist attacks, and guerrilla activity. We live with signs of rebellion all around us.

But seeds of rebellion lie within us, too, and can quickly become stubborn weeds. The subtle sin of rebellion may lie dormant for a while, but eventually it springs to life and contaminates our relationships. It may manifest itself in our opposing God's will, because we don't like what He allows to our enter own lives. It's okay with us if He blesses us, but we rebel at the first sign of adversity. Like spoiled children, we pout and whine about a dented fender or a broken finger. We get angry with God when our back acts up or our knees give out or our funds dry up or our friends let us down or our marriage breaks up or the company we work for goes belly up. We refuse to believe the promise of Romans 8:28 that "in all things God works for the good of those who love him." We fail to trust God with our present and future even though we know He has handled the past in magnificent style.

The Israelites rebelled against God in the desert. They forgot that God had protected them from the Egyptian pharaoh's cavalry and led them, dry shod through the Red Sea. They ignored the fact that He led them by a cloud during each day and a pillar of fire every night. They whined and complained, said they preferred Egypt to the desert they were passing through, and refused to enter the Promised Land when God gave them the opportunity to do so. Deuteronomy 9:7

addresses a stern rebuke to that generation of Israelites: "From the day you left Egypt until you arrived here [the land of Moab], you have been rebellious against the LORD."

Although Americans do not have a covenant relationship with God, as the Israelites did, we enjoy a rich spiritual heritage. Our founding fathers established a nation of religious freedom and identified it as "one nation under God." It speaks volumes about our in-God-we-trust beginning era that a number of rooms at Mount Vernon, President George Washington's home, display the Bible and the words of John 11:25 are inscribed on the George Washington's tomb. Today, the Bible is rejected by many Americans, read by too few, scorned by some, and ignored by too many. One Gallup survey shows that fewer than half of Americans can name the first book of the Bible, only a third know who preached the Sermon on the Mount, and a quarter can't identify what Easter celebrates.

American culture is high on technology but low on values. Many know their computer handbooks but don't know the Bible. George Gallup highlighted this tragic disregard for the Bible. "We revere the Bible, but we don't read it," he stated.

An old, decaying barge perches at the brink of Niagara Falls on the Canadian side. It had drifted down the Niagara River, swept along by the rapids, until it lodged against a rock. Those on board spent a harrowing night. They could hear the roar of the nearby falls and knew their lives were in jeopardy. At any moment, their barge could separate from the rock and plunge over the falls. Fear turned one sailor's hair gray overnight. Fortunately, the terrified sailors were rescued the next day.

No one can predict how long our nation can continue to rebel against God without being swept to judgment. But Christians can launch a rescue operation. First, we must examine our own lives. If we find such subtle sins as anger, hatred, hostility, resentment, or a spirit of rebellion, we must confess them and seek restored fellowship with God. Then we must obey Jesus in all things and throw the lifeline of salvation to a nation in peril. Our nation can be discipled in this generation, but first we must disciple ourselves, our families, and our congregations. As obedient and equipped followers of Jesus, we can reach out to our neighbors and communities with Jesus' love and teachings and ultimately blanket our nation with righteousness.

Discipleship is not an option; it's a mandate (Matthew 28:18-20). Sign on now for the greatest rescue operation in history.

> "All authority in heaven and on earth have been given to me. Therefore go and make disciples of all nations, baptizing them in the name of the Father and of the Son and of the Holy Spirit, and teaching them to obey everything I have commanded you. And surely I am with you always, to the very end of the age" (Matthew 28:18-20).

For Personal Reflection and/or Group Discussion

1. What evidence supports the view that anger is a universal problem?

2. How would you answer someone who said, "I can't help it if I lose my temper, I was born that way"?

3. How do adults occasionally throw temper tantrums?

4. What do you think is the best way to respond to an angry person?

5. How might you answer a neighbor who tells you he hates gays?

6. Is it possible to be hostile but not aggressive? Are hostile feelings as sinful as aggression? Explain your answers.

7. What advice would you give to a parent who is concerned about a son or daughter's rebellious attitude?

8. What do you think is the most effective action a follower of Jesus can take to combat moral decline in the United States?

9. How can a follower of Jesus resent wrongdoing but love the wrongdoer?

10. How does knowing that Jesus has all authority in heaven and earth encourage you to disciple others?

Chapter 7

THE SUBTLE SINS OF A LOOSE TONGUE

"**O**pen wide and say, 'ah.'"

What is the doctor looking for when he asks a patient to do that? An indication of your body health. A pinkish red color is usually normal. A yellow-coated tongue may be a tip-off to a feverish disease or a digestive problem. White, raised patches may indicate thrush, an infection caused by the fungus *candid albicans*.

The tongue also serves as a tip-off to a person's emotional and spiritual health. A distraught person may fly into a rage at the drop of a hat or withdraw into a silent, private world. An insecure person may criticize those whom he or she perceives as security threats. Someone who harbors impure thoughts may launch frequent tirades against sexual immorality. An individual who gossips may be trying to divert attention from his own faults. (When anyone points a finger at others, four fingers point back at him.) A person who berates the church may be covering his own intense need of God.

During the summer of 2001 in Colorado bears were showing up far from the mountains, where bears usually hang out, eat berries, and do whatever else bears do. Dry weather had diminished the their natural food supply, so some of them lumbered into front-range communities in search of fast food. Food discarded in garbage cans or pet food left outdoors became easy targets. Remarkably, only a few people had close encounters of the worst kind. They received bites and scratches but lived to tell their grizzly stories. The bears received tranquilizers and a free trip back to the mountains.

Bears on the loose usually want nothing to do with humans. They would rather stay clear of them. However, a bear that feels cornered by a human may attack, so the target is well advised to try to avoid an attack by backing away quietly. Turning and running only arouses a bear's hunting instinct.

A tongue on the loose constitutes a more serious danger than a bear. It wanders where it doesn't belong and intentionally inflicts harm, sometimes permanent harm.

A number of subtle sins can be traced to a loose tongue: lying, gossip, slander, stating half truths, insincerity, spreading discord, and causing factions. Most of us would never rob a bank or mug an old lady, but are we guilty of robbing a person of his or her reputation by speaking wrongfully about that person? Are we guilty of beating up someone by harsh criticism and lying?

Lying has destroyed marriages, damaged corporations, distressed families, divided congregations, discredited politicians, defamed faith, and dishonored God. It has pervaded so many areas of life that mistrust runs high. Far too many advertising claims grab our attention and pocketbooks but fail to win our lasting confidence. We buy toothpaste that doesn't live up to its promise; it doesn't make our teeth pearly white almost overnight. The magic pill or moist application doesn't relieve our muscle aches and catapult us immediately onto a tennis court as we saw happen to the 50something model in the TV commercial. We purchase a dream home and find it to be a nightmare because the building contractor lied about his workmanship or quality materials. The miracle weight-loss drink or capsule guaranteed to rid us of 10 pounds over the weekend leaves us a few dollars shorter, no lighter, and looking for the nearest fast food restaurant. The hot tip we got about a surefire moneymaking stock opportunity burns us and our money. A Classified ad urges us to send $50 to a post office box number and get back a plan for becoming rich. But the plan never arrives, or if it does, it suggests placing a similar ad in several newspapers. A furniture dealer advertises "no interest for one full year," but doesn't indicate that at the end of the year interest for the first year will be assessed. An appliance technician says our dishwasher needs a new motor, but the problem is actually only a loose wire. A telemarketer claims we have been selected to receive a $50 discount coupon toward carpet cleaning. But the caller doesn't tell us nearly everyone in the telephone directory has also been selected. Nor does the caller reveal that his company's price is $50 higher than the next highest competitor's price. A politician running for office pledges that he will always tell the truth but may say so with his fingers crossed behind his back.

Fortunately, honesty, truthfulness, and integrity have not vanished from the earth. We can still find a trustworthy politician, carpet cleaner, auto mechanic, furniture dealer, appliance technician, Classified ad, financial adviser, building contractor, manufacturers of toothpaste or pain medication, but we may need to search longer and harder than ever before.

Some lies or perceived lies are harder to forget than others, especially if the public's trust was violated. Who can forget George Bush telling the nation, "Read my lips. No new taxes." But when taxes increased, some of his political opponents accused him of lying and the read-my-lips TV clip was repeated frequently in mocking fashion. Bill Clinton stared into the TV camera and told Americans, "I never had sexual relations with that woman, Ms. Lewinsky." Although he later put a mind-boggling spin on his words, many Americans believed then and now that he lied to them.

A few years ago, a lie caused a sudden drop in sales at a popular discount department store. Someone alleged that a customer had been bitten by a cobra while handling a bolt of cloth in the domestics department. The lie insisted the customer had been transported to a hospital and nearly lost her life. According to the lie, the cobra had nested in the cloth and had arrived with it from India. Eventually the alleged incident was shown to be a hoax perpetrated by a disgruntled former customer.

Less damaging but equally sinful are so-called little lies. "The boss is not in his office," a receptionist tells a caller. "I can't come to work today. I have a terrible headache," an employee alleges as he drops a sleeve of golf balls into his pocket. "I'm going to Tony's so we can work on homework together," a middle school student tells his parents. But playing video games at Tony's hardly qualifies as homework. "That was a wonderful meal, Honey," Carl tells his wife before announcing he's going bowling with the boys.

The Bible says God hates "a lying tongue" and "a false witness who pours out lies" (Proverbs 6:16, 17, 19). Proverbs 19:5 warns: "A false witness will not go unpunished, and he who pours out lies will not go free." Those who refuse to heed this warning ought to consider the destiny of unrepentant liars. Revelation 21:8 predicts that liars "will be in the fiery lake of burning sulphur" along with such reprobates as "the vile, the murderers, the sexually immoral, those who practice the magic arts," and "the idolaters." No wonder Psalm 34:13 and 14 pleads "keep your tongue from evil and your lips from speaking lies. Turn from evil and do good; seek peace and pursue it."

Lies insult God's character but reflect the devil's character. Titus 1:2 affirms that God "does not lie." Jesus declared, "I am . . . the truth" (John 14:6). The devil, on the other hand, "is a liar and the father of lies" (John 8:44). Clearly, all who profess to love God and follow His Son Jesus should adhere to the truth and abstain from lying.

Reportedly, Petrarch, the Italian poet of great personal integrity, was summoned to court to serve as a witness. Upon seeing Petrarch at his bench, the judge closed the book and announced, "As to you, Petrarch, your word is sufficient." Every follower of Jesus should strive for that kind of reputation!

William Cullen Bryant wrote:

> *Truth, crushed to earth, shall rise again;*
> *The eternal years of God are hers;*
> *But Error, wounded, writhes in pain,*
> *And dies among his worshipers.*

Sometimes error disguises itself as a half-truth, but telling a *half-truth is also a subtle sin*. A close relative to outright lying, a half-truth consists of truth and falsehood mixed together with the intent of deceiving. A salesman may tell his boss, "I placed 50 phone calls yesterday," hoping the boss will assume he placed 50 sales calls. In reality, he placed only 30 sales calls. The other 20 were personal. A husband may tell his wife that her homemade dessert was truly a wonder, when he actually means he wondered how he could eat it. A teenager tells his parents, "I didn't mean to get home late. Sean's car broke down." Sean's car did break down, but that was a week ago and it was repaired the next day. A pharmaceutical company boasts that its anti-depressive is highly successful in helping combat depression, but it fails to mention that the anti-depressive is addictive.

The patriarch Abraham was guilty of a half-truth when he lied about his wife Sarah. He told Abimilech, king of Gerar, that Sarah was his sister (Genesis 20:2). Although Sarah was his sister (half-sister;

verse 12), Abraham concealed the fact that she was also his wife. Only the Lord's intervention kept Sarah out of Abimilech's harem.

If Abraham, "God's friend" (James 2:23), could commit the subtle sin of telling a half-truth, how alert do we need to be to the temptation to convey less than the whole truth?

Insincerity is another subtle sin that is closely aligned with lying. It occurs when we make statements we don't believe, promises we don't intend to keep, or claims we know are false. According to a recent ABC News/Beliefnet poll, 83 percent of Americans call themselves Christians. But how many of the 83 percent can back up their profession with evidence of genuine faith? It would be easy to identify oneself as a Christian simply to appear religious, respectable, and moral without being sincere. Jesus cut to the root of insincerity by asking, "Why do you call me 'Lord, Lord,' and do not do what I say" (Luke 6:46). He said further, "If you love me, you will obey what I command" (John 14:15). Sincere faith demonstrates loyalty to Jesus.

Decide for yourself whether the following situations portray the subtle sin of insincerity.

- Jack tells his wife he loves her, but he spends more time with his single friends than he does with her.

- Georgia compliments Maxine on her new dress but later tells Clara it was the ugliest dress she had ever seen.

- Gunther sells his 1992 car to a high school senior. He knows it needs an engine overhaul, new brakes, and shocks, but tells the highschooler, "This car will run great for you and save you a bundle of money. You can put what you save in repairs toward college."

- At church, Carl and Molly sing loudly, "I'll go where you want me to go, dear Lord," but they refuse to walk across the street to disciple a neighbor.

- Manuel claims his favorite hymn is "Sweet Hour of Prayer," but it has been months since he spent even five minutes in prayer.

- Knowing that Ida is facing cancer surgery, Joanna tells her,

"I'll be praying for you." However, Joanna has no intention of praying for Ida.

- Three months ago Toby promised to walk a fellow employee through a complicated software program. Although he has had time to make good on his promise, Toby has made excuses for not doing so.

- Juanita signed up as a volunteer to deliver meals to the elderly, but every time she is asked to do so, she says, "Sorry, I'm busy."

- "Good sermon. Very inspiring," Rick compliments his pastor after the worship service. Later, he calls a church board member to suggest the board reprimand the pastor for preaching such a hard-hitting sermon."

- Janelle meets a new neighbor while shopping, but fails to invite her to the weekly women's Bible study that meets at Janelle's home. The Bible study topic is "Women Discipling Women."

- In a recent conversation with Christian friends, Joy and Ray shared the opinion that bringing up children to love and serve Jesus is the highest privilege parents can have. Although they have taken their two children, ages three and five, to church, Joy and Ray have never read a Bible story to them, given them Christian toys, played Christian kids music for them, or shown them a Christian video.

The subtle sin of insincerity can pop up even in our prayers. How sincere is our interest in Rocky's search for a job if we pray simply, "Lord, bless Rocky." Are we guilty of insincerity if we say we want our nation to be discipled in this generation but rarely pray for our nation? What might happen if we sincerely prayed specifically for our leaders, local, state, and federal? "Lord, the House of Representatives will be considering an initiative next week that would allow voluntary invocations at public school graduations and sports events. Please give our Representative Sandoval the courage to vote for this initiative." Or, "Lord, Thursday the City Council plans to vote on a proposal to ban adult bookstores from operating in our community. Please help Mayor Jones and the council members cast their votes against pornography." Or, "Grant Governor Engler the wisdom and moral courage to guide our state in ways that honor You, Lord."

If you follow football, you are acquainted with statements like the following: "This team really wants to win, and they are showing it in their running game and good defense." "You know when they hit hard like that, they came here to win." "This is a blue-collar team. It practices hard and plays hard." "These guys have their game faces on." "What a disciplined team. The players know the game plan, and they are sticking with it." "Even though Nelson is hurt, he wants to stay in the game." All of these statements underscore the fact that hard-working teams are sincere about wanting to win.

But what would you say about the sincerity of a football team that arrived late for the game? preferred to sit or lie on the sidelines? refused to followed a game plan? disobeyed the coach? merely hand tackled? seldom huddled with the quarterback? dragged their feet after receiving a punt or a pass? shrugged their shoulders when the other team scored? envied their teammates' positions? never gave football a second thought after the game? resisted change? blamed each loss on the coaching staff?

Followers of Jesus are a team engaged in more than a game. We face a lifelong struggle against the devil and his evil forces. If we are sincere in our faith, we will obey our Coach, the Lord Jesus Christ, discipline ourselves, disciple others, defeat the enemy, and capture an eternal trophy. But we cannot win from the sidelines. We must put on our game face, run onto the field, follow our game plan— the Great Commission (Matthew 28:18-20)—use our spiritual gifts in cooperation with our teammates, and "run" with the teachings of Jesus until we reach the end zone.

Occasionally, the public hears disturbing reports of team discord. Players badmouth one another. Their slander and gossip cause bitterness and resentment in the locker room and pathetic play on the gridiron or court. It takes a Herculean effort on the part of the coaching staff and sincere reconciliation of the parties involved to unify the team and restore the focus on its mission. But families and congregations, too, may experience factions and discord due to *the subtle sins of slander and gossip.* Nothing severs relationships faster than a sharp tongue.

A father or mother commit the subtle sin of slander when they tell a son or daughter, "You will never amount to anything. You're just plain dumb." By defaming the child, the thoughtless parent builds a wall between them. It is not uncommon to hear a parent say, "I don't know what to do with my teenage kids. They are so bad and lazy. I will be so glad when they get old enough to move into their own place."

Of course, some kids slander their parents. They say things like, "My parents are totally out of it"; "Mom and Dad are just plain boring"; "My dad has to be the worst father in the world"; "I hate it when my friends meet my mother. She dresses like a nerd."

No one needs a ton of hard data to recognize that the American family needs help. A trip to the supermarket provides enough evidence of a rift in family relationships. Little children talk back to Mom, and Mom screams back at them. By the time they reach the check-out counter their heated arguing has melted the ice cream and their bitter tone has curdled the milk. By contrast, well-behaved children under the control of a loving parent seem to be a rare treat. Small wonder that so many parents and teens speak badly about one another. The feud has been festering for at least 10 years!

Envisioning a more harmonious America, Martin Luther King, Jr. delivered his famous "I Have a Dream" speech. Obedient followers of Jesus can share an even better, more authoritative message with America. It is God's "I Have a Plan" message. Instead of slander, God prescribes respect, love, patience, and forgiveness. Here are just a few of His prescribed instructions for a happy and productive family life:

> "Children, obey your parents in the Lord, for this right. Honor your father and mother . . . that it may go well with you and that you may enjoy long life upon the earth. Fathers, do not exasperate your children; instead, bring them up in the training and instruction of the Lord." (Ephesians 6:1-4).

> "Love the Lord your God with all your heart and with all your soul and with all your strength. These

commandments . . . are to be upon your hearts. Impress them on your children. Talk about them when you sit at home and when you walk along the road, when you lie down and when you get up" (Deuteronomy 6:5-7).

"Let love and faithfulness never leave you; bind them around your neck, write them on the tablet of your heart" (Proverbs 3:3).

"Whoever loves discipline loves knowledge, but he who hates correction is stupid" (Proverbs 12:1).

"A wise son heeds his father's instruction" (Proverbs 13:1).

"A gentle answer turns away wrath, but a harsh word stirs up anger" (Proverbs 15:1).

"Train a child in the way he should go, and when he is old he will not turn from it" (Proverbs 22:6).

"Love is patient, love is kind . . . it is not rude . . . it is not easily angered, it keeps no record of wrongs" (1 Corinthians 13:4, 5).

Summer in western states can be scorching hot, running the fire danger into the "Extreme" category. A carelessly thrown match or cigarette can ignite thousands of acres of forest land into an inferno. Houses in the path of a blaze can explode like fireworks, and wildlife caught in the fire have little or no chance of surviving. Only charred stumps, scarred ground, and torched rocks remain to tell the devastating results stemming from such a little thing as a carelessly thrown match or cigarette.

A careless word dropped from a loose tongue can also produce devastating results. Many destroyed reputations, depleted congregations, distrustful associates, and damaged relationships lie in the wake of fires caused by *the subtle sins of lying, slander, gossip, half truths, insincerity, discord, and factions.* The apostle James wrote: "The tongue also is a fire, a world of evil among the parts of the body. It corrupts the whole person, sets the whole course of his life on fire, and is itself set on fire by hell" (James 3:6).

The luster of silver shows well against a dark background. Followers of Jesus can repent of misspoken words and ask the Lord to help them use kind and loving words to disciple their family members, neighbors, and the nation. When that happens, the contrast between light and darkness will be striking and we will understand more fully the truth that "a word aptly spoken is like apples of gold in settings of silver" (Proverbs 25:11).

For Personal Reflection and/or Group Discussion

1. What incidents of lying have you encountered recently? How have these incidents affected you?

2. Which do you believe is more dangerous, a total lie or a half truth? Why?

3. What deceptive advertising have you witnessed recently? What should be the chief characteristics of advertising placed by a company owned by a follower of Jesus?

4. What similarities do you see between a successful football team and a team of obedient disciples?

5. How can parents train their children to speak honestly and kindly?

6. Do you think TV or the movies or both condone or even promote bad language? Explain.

7. How would you rank gossip among believers? more common than among unbelievers? about the same? not as common as among unbelievers? Explain.

8. How can a congregation address the problem of insincere worship?

9. How might kind words prevent neighborhood squabbles?

10. What kinds of words should a follower of Jesus avoid in writing a letter to the editor.

Chapter 8

WHO'S MINDING YOUR MIND?

No, BMI is not an automobile; it's something else, and everyone has it. However, many of us would like to have less of it. BMI stands for body-mass index. If you want to know what your BMI is, divide your weight by your height. An index of 25 or more is the cutoff between normal and overweight. A BMI above 30 indicates obesity.

If you think the United States is getting crowded, you may be right. The population is expanding, not only in numbers but also in girth. Almost 61 percent of American adults are overweight. Alarmingly, about one out of every four overweight Americans is obese.

Obesity is a worldwide problem. More than a billion people on Planet Earth are overweight. Too many calories and too little exercise seem to be expanding waistlines and loosening chin lines. Mass consumption of junk food only compounds the problem. Since we are what we eat, we shouldn't be surprised to see more people shaped like double-cheeseburgers than celery stalks.

What we feed our minds can be a problem too. Stuffing the mind with unhealthful thoughts has a detrimental effect on relationships, attitudes, and behavior. A diet of impure thoughts is sure to produce negative relationships, hurtful attitudes, and immoral behavior. Jesus grouped evil thoughts, adultery, and immorality together (Matthew 15:19). But isn't it okay to engage in immoral fantasies as long as you don't commit immoral deeds? Some people would answer yes, but the Lord isn't one of them. Proverbs 15:26 reports: "The LORD detests the thoughts of the wicked, but those of the pure are pleasing to him." *The subtle sin of immoral fantasies* corrupts the life as surely as stubborn weeds destroy a garden. The apostle Paul reminded the followers of the Lord at Ephesus that their lives used to reflect the thinking and conduct of an evil culture. At that time, he said, they gratified the cravings of their sinful nature, "following its desires and thoughts" (Ephesians 2:3).

OVERCOMING Subtle Sins

Computer technology has enhanced communication and made access to information almost as rapid as a click. But it has also opened the door of the mind to a world of immoral fantasies. Thousands of pornographic web sites lure even youth and children to a dark, indecent, lewd, vile thought life. Chat rooms, too, may lure users into immoral fantasies and even into sexual liaisons.

Even Christians can become victims of immoral fantasies and sexual immorality. Enrolling in a seminary or joining its staff does not provide immunity for anyone whose mind is open to immoral fantasies. Occasionally, but infrequently, a professor is fired or a student is expelled for accessing pornography on the Internet. More frequently, a marriage is wrecked by an Internet romance.

Earl was regarded as an ardent believer. He was married, the father of five young children, a graduate of a Christian college, a successful businessman, and a Bible study leader for his church. But he entered a chat room one day and met Pamela. The two soon discovered they shared common interests and compatible personalities. Before long, they exchanged photos of each other and fell into an electronic love affair. When Earl suggested Pamela meet him in a neutral city he would be visiting on business, she agreed. The two met, had a brief affair, and returned to their homes. However, their homes could never be the same again. Eventually, the affair became public and both lost their marriages and their interest in each other. They want to reconcile with their spouses and live again with their children, but the chasm between them and their families seems impassable.

Immoral fantasies and impure thoughts are not linked only to a bad use of the Internet. They are often fanned by television, videos, and movies. Unless a person exercises a discriminating choice, he or she may view sexually offensive images and hear crude language while sitting in the family room or in a theater. Even many TV commercials seem to rely on bare skin to sell anything from soft drinks to soap bars. Often a parent must keep a fast finger on the remote or suffer the embarrassment of having the children exposed to offensive material.

Studies have shown that most American children watch between three and six hours of television per day, often unsupervised by their parents. Furthermore, psychologists suggest that inappropriate TV subject matter can negatively affect the children's thoughts and actions. It stands to reason, therefore, that parents would be well advised to take such actions as removing TV sets from their children's bedrooms, disallowing TV watching during mealtimes, selecting only wholesome programs, and making appropriate books readily available.

Of course, a good parental example is the best method of safeguarding a child's sense of morals. Since children usually follow in a parent's footsteps, the parent should make sure he or she is walking in the right direction. King David must have been concerned about the direction of his life and the impact it would have on his sons and daughters when he prayed: "Search me, O God, and know my heart; test me and know my anxious thoughts. See if there is any offensive way in me, and lead me in the way everlasting" (Psalm 139:23, 24). In another psalm, he expressed confidence in God's Word as life's perfect guidebook. He wrote: "Blessed are they whose ways are blameless, who walk according to the law of the LORD. Blessed are they who keep his statutes and seek him with all their heart. They do nothing wrong; they walk in his ways" (Psalm 119:1-3).

A glass of dirty water can be transformed into a glass of clean water by using a method called displacement. Simply run clean water into the glass until it displaces all the dirty water. Similarly, unclean thoughts can be displaced by pure thoughts. As we fill our minds with the teachings of Scripture, right thinking will displace wrong thinking. Psalm 119:9 and 11 highlight this formula: "How can a young man keep his way pure? By living according to your word . . . I have hidden your word in my heart that I might not sin against you." Philippians 4:8 instructs: " . . . whatever is true, whatever is noble, whatever is right, whatever is pure, whatever is lovely, whatever is admirable—if anything is excellent or praiseworthy—think about such things."

Ephesians 4:22, 23 challenges followers of Jesus to discard thoughts and actions associated with an immoral and unrighteous lifestyle. This passage challenges: "You were taught, with regard to your former way of life, to put off your old self, which is being corrupted by its deceitful desires; to be made new in the attitude of your minds; and to put on the new self, created to be like God in true righteousness and holiness."

Of course, immoral fantasies are not the only subtle sin that attack the mind. *Fear is another subtle sin* that invades the mind. It is the opposite of faith. Faith rests in God's love, wisdom, and power. Fear finds no rest. A fearful person looks at the world around him, sees a sagging economy, rising prices, expanding conflicts, shrinking security, and an uncertain future, and becomes distressed. A person who has faith may see similar circumstances but does not fear because he looks above the circumstances to the Lord who has everything under control.

The fact that the *Left Behind* book series has sold more than 40 million copies probably says something about widespread fear of the future. Many readers, disturbed by world conditions, especially those in the Middle East, have turned to the *Left Behind* books to learn what lies ahead.

When interviewed on Larry King Live, *Left Behind* authors Jerry Jenkins and Tim LaHaye shared the good news that Jesus Christ will return someday to remove believers from this troubled earth before conditions reach their worst.

In the growing up years of the film industry, brief serials often accompanied feature movies. Typically, a serial episode would run about 10 minutes and end with the hero trapped in an impossible situation. He might be in cave and unable to get out because fallen rocks blocked the exit. To add to the misery, rushing water swirled around the hero's feet, then his knees, then his waist, and then his shoulders. THE END. To find out if the hero escaped, theatergoers would have to return to see the next episode. Those who saw the next episode could tell those who missed it how it all turned out.

Followers of Jesus enjoy a peace-producing knowledge of how it will all turn out. The Bible pulls the curtain of the future aside and offers us a preview. It shows we have nothing to fear, because God is in control.

Fear enslaves; faith liberates. Fear is negative; faith is positive. Fear takes away a zest for life; faith gives a zest for life. Fear rejects what the Bible promises; faith accepts its promises. Fear turns away from Jesus' command to make disciples; faith embraces the challenge.

Those who put their faith in Jesus and follow Him know experientially the truth Paul taught in 2 Timothy 1:7: "God did not give us a spirit of timidity, but a spirit of power, of love and self-discipline."

The subtle sin of skepticism and unbelief are related to fear. The skeptic thinks, *I dare not trust the Lord. I must not commit myself to a life of obedience to Jesus. He may disappoint me. I will rely on my own intelligence and abilities.* The unbeliever simply rejects the light God has revealed to him. His unbelief is as foolish as that of a person who chooses to stumble in a dark room rather than turn on a light switch.

Our nation includes an alarming number of skeptics and unbelievers. They work next to us. They live in our neighborhood. They teach or study in our colleges and universities. They counsel in our institutions. They report the news. They write books and magazine articles. They even attend church!

Upon arriving home for summer vacation, a college student stood in the backyard garden alongside his father. "Dad, he said, I won't be going to church with you and Mother this summer. I no longer believe in God. College has enlightened me to the fact that either God doesn't exist, or if He does, He can't be trusted to handle my life.

"Dad, see this pumpkin vine beside the big oak tree we're standing under? If God created everything, He made a big mistake. Huge pumpkins are hanging from this skinny vine, but tiny acorns are hanging from the sturdy oak tree. If I had made the world, I would have put the pumpkins on oak trees and acorns on skinny vines."

Just then, a heavy breeze shook the oak tree, and an acorn landed squarely on the college skeptic's head.

Startled, he continued, "Dad, maybe God does things the right way, after all."

Skeptics and unbelievers aren't faith-free, of course. It takes faith to believe that the universe came into existence as a result of exploding gases or that all forms of life originated from a single cell. It takes faith in oneself to believe he or she can navigate successfully through life without divine assistance. And it takes faith to board an airplane or to trust a surgeon to remove your appendix or an elevator to carry you several stories up and down in a building. It also takes faith to swallow a prescribed pill or to eat in a restaurant. So why are skeptics unwilling to follow Jesus' instructions to "trust in God; trust also in me" (John 14:1)?

Trusting in Jesus means, among other things, obeying His command to make disciples. He has promised disciple-makers that all authority in heaven and earth belongs to Him and He has guaranteed His presence with us to the very end of the age. Calling oneself a Christian while refusing to disciple others is perhaps the worst kind of skepticism.

Addiction is another subtle sin that we need to confront, repent of, and forsake. No one can live in these modern times without being keenly aware of the horrors of drug addiction. Lives wrecked by drugs challenge our social and medical agencies and tear at our hearts. Perhaps nothing is more heart-rending than to see a newborn baby writhe and twitch in anguish because he or she suffers a heroin addiction acquired from the addicted mother. Prenatal exposure to heroin may predispose babies to such physical and psychological challenges as a smaller than normal heart size, brain deficiency, gastrointestinal abnormalities, nervous system dysfunctions, respiratory problems, and seizures. In view of the effects of heroin on babies, it is especially staggering to learn that there are nearly 600,000 addicts in the U.S..

Our nation's youth, too, have been victimized by illegal drugs. The National Institute on Drug Use reports that the number of youth who have used illegal drugs increased 6,000 percent in the second half of the twenty-first century. Many public schools post "Drug Free Zone" signs at their perimeters. Border Police confiscate tons of illegal drugs smuggled into our country. Drug busts occur frequently in our urban and suburban neighborhoods. Marijuana blooms in backyards, and meth labs bubble in basements and bathrooms. Some motorists are pulled over for traffic violations but end up in prison because illegal drugs are found in their cars or trucks. Crack cocaine exchanges hands on street corners and hangouts, and club drugs sneak into rave parties and rock concerts. The drug ecstasy has swept too many teenagers not only into euphoria but also into eternity.

We all know the tobacco industry has been in the cross hairs. Cigarette smoking has been blamed for such diseases as lung cancer, heart disease, and emphysema. But alcohol is also a drug. Its abuse has flooded Skid Row, impoverished families, contributed to spousal abuse, sparked fights, led to murders, and resulted in traffic injuries and fatalities. Recently, the abuse of alcohol by college students was singled out by the medical community as a major problem on our nation's college campuses.

Why are so many youth and adults addicted to drugs? Likely, peer pressure deserves part of the blame, but each individual user must shoulder most of the blame. Bad choices are, after all, choices. No one is forced to smoke pot or snort cocaine or chugalug beer. However, parents must also share the blame if they set a bad example or fail to educate their children about the dangers of drug use. A mother who downs cocktails like there's no tomorrow may be robbing her children of a future. A father who heads for the liquor cabinet as soon as he returns home from the office teaches his kids that a quick fix is the only way to handle stress.

Addiction to drugs is not the only kind of addiction. Some men and women are addicted to work. These workaholics never have enough time for family or leisure, because they have strapped themselves to an office chair or sales chart. Foodaholics are addicts too. For them, the DASH diet means dashing to the refrigerator during every commercial, dashing to the nearest all-you-can eat buffet, dashing to a donut shop, dashing to an ice cream store, and dashing to a candy vending machine during the afternoon break. Some Americans are sexaholics. Their minds dwell on sexual images, and their spending supports pornography. Gambling can be another powerful addiction. Twenty years ago, Americans spent about $17 billion per year on legal gambling. Today, the figure tops $550 billion. In 1988 only Nevada allowed gambling casinos. Today, 22 states have casinos. An estimated 5 to 10 million Americans fall into the category of compulsive gamblers.

Even Christians are not immune to addictive habits. The subtle sin of addiction may strike anyone, but a strong commitment to Jesus Christ affords unbeatable protection. Followers of Jesus learn from Scripture that the body belongs to God and is the temple of the Holy Spirit (1 Corinthians 6:19, 20). We understand that God instructs us to practice self-control (9:24-27) and gives us the power to resist temptation. We realize the power of a good example (1 Timothy 4:12; 1 Peter 2:21), and know that God has called us to lead a holy life (1 Peter 1:15, 16).

Someone asked Abraham Lincoln about his candidacy for the office of President. Lincoln replied that he did not fear his opponent

Breckinridge, because he was a southerner and the North would not support him. Nor did he fear Douglas, because the South would not vote for him. "But," said Lincoln, "there is a man named Lincoln, of whom I am very much afraid. If I am defeated, it will be by that man."

Our own worst enemy may be ourselves. In our weakness, we may open our minds to immoral thoughts and impurity, fear, skepticism and unbelief, and addiction. But we can be victors instead of victims. Repentance, submission to the Holy Spirit, and renewed obedience to Jesus' teachings and commandments can purify our minds and empower our words and deeds. We can be credible disciplers of others, used by the Lord to "preach good news to the poor . . . to bind up the brokenhearted, to proclaim freedom for the captives and release from darkness for the prisoners" (Isaiah 61:1).

For Personal Reflection and/or Group Discussion

1. Why do you agree or disagree that a pure mind is essential to successful Christian living.

2. What guidelines should a believer follow in using the Internet?

3. How might the Internet be used to disciple our nation?

4. What kinds of TV programs are beneficial? Why?

5. What kinds of TV programs are harmful? Why?

6. How would you respond to an alcoholic who excuses his addiction by insisting that Jesus drank wine?

7. How do you feel about the medicinal use of marijuana?

8. If your community launched a referendum to allow casino gambling, how would you vote? Why?

9. How can a commitment to Jesus drive away fear?

10. How can a commitment to Jesus liberate an addict?

Chapter 9

THE UNBEARABLE WEIGHT OF A CHIP ON THE SHOULDER

According to Greek mythology, the chief god, Zeus, forced Atlas, a Titan, to carry the heavens on his shoulders as punishment for joining the Titans in a revolt against the gods. How different is the true God, our heavenly Father! The psalmist testified, "Praise be to the Lord, to God our Savior, who daily bears our burdens" (Psalm 68:19). Jesus, the Son of God, extends an invitation to "come to me, all you who are weary and burdened." He promises, "I will give you rest" (Matthew 11:19).

Would it surprise you to learn that a chip on the shoulder is one of life's heaviest loads? It reflects *the subtle sin of bitterness* and left unconfessed it can wear down even the most physically fit. Bitterness brings heaviness to the human spirit and crushes the soul. It robs us of joy and peace. It makes us unfit to live with ourselves, sours our personality, and renders us unattractive to others. Bitterness is too heavy a load to carry for a single day, but some poor souls carry it for a lifetime.

Bitterness may be directed at God. A couple may harbor bitterness toward God because they endured a miscarriage. A teenager may be bitter toward God because Mom died of cancer. Another may be bitter because Mom and Dad divorced. A job loss, a disability, a broken engagement, a marriage gone bad, poverty, unattractive physical characteristics, and a thousand other issues are cited as reasons for being bitter toward God. But are they reasons or excuses?

Because we live in an imperfect world—a world marred by evil— bad things happen. Sometimes some very bad things happen to very good people. The rain falls on both the righteous and the unrighteous, Jesus affirmed (Matthew 5:45). A tornado may destroy a church as well as a tavern. A faulty-wired house owned by Christians may burn to the ground. Cancer strikes without partiality; some of Jesus' most devoted followers may spend their final days on earth in a hospice.

We cannot explain why God allows tragedy to invade our lives or the lives of our loved ones. Why me? Why my wife? Why my husband? Why my mother? Why my dad? Why my son? Why my daughter? These questions are troubling, but they need not drive us to bitterness.

An Illinois pastor, his wife, and several of their children were traveling on an interstate highway north of Chicago, when part of a truck's frame broke off, struck their van, and ripped into the gas tank. The exploding gas tank turned the van into an inferno, severely burned the pastor and his wife, and took the lives of all the children on board. In subsequent interviews the pastor and his wife showed no bitterness, spoke about the reality of heaven and their hope of joining their children there someday, and demonstrated compassion for the truck driver.

A missionary pilot and a missionary couple with their young son and baby daughter were flying in Peru above the Amazon River when life took a tragic turn. Mistaking the missionary plane for one carrying illegal drugs, a Peruvian fighter plane riddled it with bullets, forcing it to crash in the piranha-infested Amazon River. The mother and baby perished. The pilot and the father and son sustained injuries but survived. The horrendous incident received international attention, including a U.S. network television interview with the father and son. The interview gave Americans a glimpse into missionary life and an opportunity to learn how faith in the Lord triumphs over bitterness. Although both father and son missed the other family members, they told the interviewer their loved ones were in heaven and they held no bitterness toward the Peruvian fighter pilot.

Indeed, earth holds no sorrow that heaven cannot heal! Our heavenly Father, who is "the God of all comfort" (2 Corinthians 1:3), supplies peace even when we lay the body of a loved one to rest. We know Jesus is preparing heaven for those who love Him (John 14:1, 2). He is also preparing those who love Him for heaven. This present life is fleeting; the next is eternal. When a Christian loved one dies, he or she steps into heaven. Pain and suffering, disappointment and discouragement, trials and tears, temptations and tragedy are gone forever. Bliss, peace, rewards, rich fellowship, beauty, joy and a plethora of other blessings adorn heaven. By focusing on our heavenly Father and our eternal home we can keep bitterness away from our minds and hearts.

The Old Testament introduces a man who could easily have been bitter. His name was Job. When we first meet Job, we learn that he was a wealthy rancher. His spread was pre-Texan era but at least Texan size. His livestock covered the range, and his ranch hands were numerous. He and his wife headed a large family. They had ten adult children, seven sons and three daughters, who lived in their own homes. The Book of Job distinguishes Job as "the greatest man among all the people of the East" (1:3).

But Job's greatness was due only in part to his success as a rancher. He was a man of God and an outstanding family man. The first verse of the Book of Job describes him as blameless, upright, and one who reverenced God and shunned evil. Every day, when the sun began to rise over the ranch, Job worshiped God with a burned offering on behalf of each of his children (1:5).

So what happened that could have made Job bitter?

Plenty!

Satan appeared before God and accused Job of serving God only because God had prospered him. Whether in ancient times or our postmodern era, it certainly is sinful to serve God only for what we can get from Him. Although we should be grateful for all He gives us, our hearts ought to be focused on the Giver instead of the gifts. But Job's motive for worshiping and serving God was pure: He reverenced God.

"If you wipe out everything he has, Job will curse you," Satan hissed.

"Very well, then," the LORD answered, "everything he has is in your hands, but on the man himself do not lay a finger" (Job 1:12).

That's what Satan was waiting to hear. Like a bulldog after a bone, he darted from the presence of the Lord to rip into Job's life.

The test was under way. Would Job become bitter and curse God at the first sign of trouble?

No, not at the first sign of trouble, not at the last sign of trouble, and not at any of the signs between the first and the last! Job did not understand why each trial struck, but his faith remained strong.

Satan was relentless. He destroyed Job's livestock, delivered Job's servants into the hands of marauders, and killed Job's sons and daughters. He was smart enough to let Job's wife live, because she would later advise Job to curse God and die (2:9).

Upon receiving reports of tragedy wave upon wave, Job was grief-stricken. He fell to the ground, not to berate God but to bless Him. He said, " . . . The LORD gave and the LORD has taken away; may the name of the LORD be praised" (1:21).

But Satan wasn't finished with Job. He appeared again before God, claiming that Job would surely curse God if He took away Job's health. As soon as God granted Satan permission to afflict Job's body without killing him, Satan was off and running (2:6, 7).

By the time Satan ended his assault on Job's health, Job had endured painful, pus-filled sores all over his body, disfigurement, nightmares, halitosis, excessive weight loss, fever, boils, and painful bones (perhaps bone cancer). To make matters worse three "friends" visited Job and told him his troubles were due to sin in his life.

Still, Job retained his faith. He even expressed the confidence that a far better life awaited him beyond the grave because he would see his Redeemer face to face (19:25-27). What he didn't know was that a better life awaited him on this side of the grave, after the trials. God rewarded Job's faith by giving him twice as much as he had before the trials, his friends' acknowledgment that he was righteousness, seven sons and three beautiful daughters, and a long and prosperous life (see Job 42:7-16).

By faith, Job had chosen not to be bitter against God, his wife, and his friends. He made the right choice—one that is available to each of us—and God honored him for making it.

Job questioned his trials, but he didn't question God. Ultimately, he learned what we, too, can learn: (1) God allows trials to enter our lives for His glory and our good; (2) He designs trials to make us better, not bitter; (3) Nothing strikes us that takes Him by surprise or imposes on us more than we can endure; (4) His grace is sufficient for every trial (2 Corinthians 12:9).

Fanny Crosby, who wrote so many inspiring hymns, never let her blindness block her view of the Lord as gracious, loving, merciful, and just. Her gratitude for who He is and what He does spilled from her heart in a flood of praiseful, joyful music. She experienced His presence as she lived by faith, and like Job, she anticipated seeing Him when she entered heaven. In her hymn, "Saved by Grace," she wrote:

"Some day the silver cord will break,
　　And I no more as now shall sing;
But O, the joy when I shall wake
　　Within the palace of the King!

"And I shall see Him face to face,
　　And tell the story—Saved by grace;
And I shall see Him face to face,
　　And tell the story—Saved by grace."

The subtle sin of bitterness may be directed toward people as well as God. The present world seems to breed bitterness. For decades Protestants and Catholics in Northern Ireland have clashed in a bitter struggle. Shootings, beatings, and bombings have claimed lives, divided neighborhoods in Belfast, and shattered families. Children on their way to school have been pelted with insults and even homemade bombs. In the '60s bitter factions tore American cities apart and hurled accusations at one another. College campuses, too, felt the anger of angry, bitter demonstrators. Our government was maligned by Vietnam war protesters, and many returning Vietnam veterans became bitter because they felt disrespected and unappreciated by so many of their countrymen.

Bitterness marred the 2001 World Conference Against Racism, held in Durban, South Africa. African and European countries clashed over the issue of slavery. European countries rejected the African nations' call for an apology for the Europeans' past enslavement of Africans. Arab nations, bitter against Israel, tried to depict Israel as racist for its conduct toward Palestine. In protest of the Arab nations' effort, the United States recalled its delegation.

The workplace can also be a seedbed of bitterness. A negative glance, a harsh word, an uncooperative attitude, a poor work ethic can sow bitterness in a work area and even spread it across departments. And who hasn't heard about some dismissed employee taking out his bitterness by returning to his former place of employment and gunning down whoever happens to be in his line of fire?

A job site is not the only habitat frequented by bitterness; it even attends church. There, it usually assumes its most subtle form. Worshipers may sing, "We are not divided. All one body, we" or "Blest be the tie that binds our hearts in Christian love," while bitter feelings toward one another churn inside them. They may know the Scripture verse that proclaims, "How good and pleasant it is when brothers live together in unity" (Psalm 133:1), but fail to experience its truth. They may hear a sermon about making "every effort to keep the unity of the Spirit in the bond of peace" (Ephesians 4:3), but listen with arms crossed and minds closed. They may believe in burying the hatchet, but they know exactly where they would like to bury it!

The Lord knows a bitter heart is a barren heart. Like dry, hard ground that resists fruit-producing seeds, a bitter heart resists the Holy Spirit's effort to produce the fruit of love, joy, peace, patience, kindness, goodness, faithfulness, gentleness and self-control" (Galatians 5:22, 23). Bitterness, therefore, offends the Lord, but it also hurts oneself. Understandably, the Lord commands us to "get rid of all bitterness" (Ephesians 4:31), replacing it with kindness and compassion (verse 32).

Followers of Jesus must clear their hearts of bitterness. They must repent of this subtle sin in order to disciple themselves and then disciple others. They need to humble themselves, confess their bitterness, and covenant with God to obey all of Jesus' teachings, including His command to "bless those who curse you, pray for those who mistreat you" (Luke 6:28). This is a tall order, but the Lord "gives grace to the humble" (James 4:6).

Worshipers at a Communion service observed a clear illustration of what it means to humble oneself and empty the heart of bitterness. Just as the pastor was beginning the service, a tall, muscular Hispanic worshiper asked permission to address the congregation. Permission granted, he approached the Communion Table and faced the congregation. "I'm visiting this church for the first time," he began. "I did not go to my own church today, because I have bitter feelings about my pastor. He said something recently that hurt me, even though what he said came from the Bible. I do not want to take Communion without confessing this bitterness and asking the Lord to forgive me. I will ask my pastor to forgive me too."

The contrite man took his seat again and participated in the Communion service with a renewed spirit.

Closely related to bitterness is *the subtle sin of unforgiveness.* Bitterness lingers in the mind and heart of the person who says, "I can forgive, but I will never forget." A wrong remembered is a wrong unforgiven. Jesus set the highest standard for forgiveness. When Peter asked him how often he should forgive an offender, Jesus answered, "Seventy-seven times" (Matthew 18:22).

The Gospels almost shout the undeserved forgiveness Jesus extended to so many when He lived in Palestine. "Take heart, son," He told a paralytic, "your sins are forgiven" (Matthew 9:2). He also pronounced forgiveness to a woman burdened with many sins (Luke 7:47. 48). Comforting an adulterous woman whom He had saved from mob execution, Jesus said, " . . . neither do I condemn you . . . Go now and leave your life of sin" (John 8:11). Even when He experienced the excruciating pain of being crucified, Jesus' love prompted Him to pray for His enemies, "Father, forgive them, for they do not know what they are doing" (Luke 23:34). Then, just before committing His spirit into His Father's hands, Jesus pardoned the repentant thief who was dying on a cross next to His. He promised: "I tell you the truth, today you will be with me in paradise" (verse 43).

The dying thief soon learned that only forgiven people enter heaven. Because everyone is imperfect, flawed by sin, and guilty of transgressing God's laws, the only road to heaven begins at the Cross. On the Cross, the only sinless human being died for sinners. The apostle Peter wrote, "For Christ died for sins once for all, the right-eous for the unrighteous, to bring you to God" (1 Peter 3:18). All who believe on Jesus as having risen from tomb after paying the penalty their sins deserved receive full and lasting forgiveness and assurance of heaven (John 3:16, 31; Romans 3:23-26; 4:25; 1 Corinthians 15:3, 4).

When God forgives our sins, He forgets them forever. Isaiah 43:25 reports His words: "I, even I, am he who blots out your transgressions, for my own sake, and remembers your sins no more." This is the kind of forgiveness Jesus' followers are instructed to extend to one another. Colossians 3:13 commands, " . . . forgive whatever grievances you may have against one another. Forgive as the Lord forgave you."

Sometimes children show a depth of understanding about spiritual truth that some adults may never attain. When asked what forgiveness is, a boy replied, "It is the fragrance flowers give after getting stepped on." That's precisely the kind of fragrance followers of Jesus need to share with members of their families; the people they worship with;

their neighbors across the street; behind them, and next to them; their co-workers; and society at large. Unlike forgiveness, bitterness and unforgiveness are obnoxious weeds that need to be uprooted and destroyed.

For Personal Reflection and/or Group Discussion:

1. How does bitterness affect personality?

2. How might bitterness affect one's career? marriage?

3. How do you explain the fact that tragedies often strike Christians?

4. How would you respond to the question, "Where was God when my two-year-old daughter died?"

5. What are a few of the best things about following Jesus closely today?

6. What are a few of the best things about heaven?

7. What signs of bitterness do you see in international relations?

8. What signs of bitterness do you see in work relations?

9. How can you, as a follower of Jesus, help erase the bitterness you see around you?

10. How will you extend forgiveness today?

Chapter 10

SLEEPING IN THE SON

"Lazy Bones, sleepin' in the sun,
How do you expect to get your day's work done?"

Maybe these words of an old song should be sung in church. After all, more than 2,000 years have passed since Jesus authorized and commanded His followers to make disciples of all nations, but much of the world has little or no knowledge of Jesus. Even thousands of men and women in the United States have yet to hear about Jesus and the wonderful life He offers. How can this doleful situation exist in a nation of 350,000 churches claiming to be Christian? The answer must lie in part in the fact that many who claim to believe on Jesus suffer biblical illiteracy. With only a trace of Bible knowledge, they are ignorant of Jesus' teachings about discipleship. We must also face the startling, but real, possibility that many believers are sleeping in the Son. They know what Jesus, the Son of God, has commanded His followers to do, but they have taken on the posture of couch potatoes. They wear the uniform of a Christian soldier, but their boots and the knees of their pants show no signs of wear. However, the seat of their pants is almost worn through. Their issued weapon, the Bible, which is the sword of the Spirit (Ephesians 6:17), lies on a table collecting dust. They slumber. Their hands are folded, and their eyes are closed.

A number of symptoms suggest the church at large is the church asleep. *The subtle sin of laziness* is one of those symptoms of this sleeping sickness. A lazy military recruit finds boot camp unpleasant, but he must shake off his laziness, follow commands, and undergo rigorous training before he can be of valuable service to his country. Similarly, a follower of the Lord must renounce laziness, and obey the commandments of Jesus, the Commander-in-Chief. But repenting of the subtle sin of laziness is simply the first step in serving Jesus as a faithful discipler of others. We must stay alert to discipling opportunities. "Watch and pray," Jesus instructed (Matthew 26:41).

September 11, 2001, will be remembered by all Americans as a day of infamy, more shameful and murderous than even Pearl Harbor, the first day of infamy. When terrorists crashed commercial planes into the World Trade Center towers and the Pentagon, 9-11-'01, some news commentators referred to the sneak attacks as "the second Pearl Harbor." Both the 1941 and 2001 catastrophes stunned our nation but cemented our collective resolve to recover and to punish and disable the perpetrators.

Recoiling at the sight of the hijacked planes broadsiding the WTC towers and Pentagon and witnessing the towers' collapse and the Pentagon's fiery devastation, millions of Americans knew a catastrophic breech of security had occurred. But what was it? Had airport security let down its guard? After all, it had been 10 years since a plane was hijacked in the United States. Had our nation lulled itself into thinking, "Terrorism happens in far-off countries. It can never happen here"?

Unfortunately, it sometimes takes a tragedy to wake us up and put us to work so a similar tragedy doesn't befall us. Commenting on the horrific terrorist attack on America, 9-11-'01, numerous government officials said, "This is a wakeup call for America."

Does the church in America need a wakeup call? Moral and spiritual tragedies exist all around our places of worship and Christian homes—even in some of our Christian homes. The family is under attack; our schools suffer from a lack of respect for authority, truancy, the mistaken notion that the Bible must be banned from the classroom, evolutionary and humanistic philosophies, lack of parental support, and violence. Our cities try to cope with gang-banging, graffiti, drug traffic, vandalism, poverty, and overcrowded jails. Even our rural areas experience problems similar to those confronting our cities.

In response to the New York City and Washington, D.C. tragedies, President Bush assured the nation that we will hunt down and punish those who struck us. "We will make no distinction between those who committed these acts and those who harbor them," he promised. Clearly, America showed a resolve to act.

How will the church respond to the moral and spiritual tragedies that intensify while so many lazy believers slumber? How will you respond? Will we show a resolve to act? Just as a single spark is capable of igniting a huge fire, so one believer—you?—is capable of setting the church ablaze with zeal to disciple our nation.

Billy Sunday, the former baseball star turned evangelist, was known for speaking directly. In a sermon, he described many of Jesus' followers as "too fat to run and too weak to fight." If he were alive and preaching today, he might add, " . . . and too lazy to work." However, it is not too late for the church to heed the call to "always give yourselves fully to the work of the LORD, because you know that your labor in the LORD is not in vain" (1 Corinthians 15:58).

Although the subtle sin of laziness has a direct, negative effect on discipling of our nation, it has indirect, negative effects as well. If a professed follower of Jesus is lazy in the workplace, his co-workers will likely tune him out when he tells them they need Jesus. An able-bodied Christian dad, who is too lazy to get a job or hold a job, sends a wrong message to his family and neighbors. He needs to take to heart the indictment given in 2 Thessalonians 3:10: "If a man will not work, he shall not eat."

The Book of Proverbs almost bursts with verses opposing the subtle sin of laziness. Here are just a few:

> "A little sleep, a little slumber, a little folding of the hands to rest—and poverty will come on you like a bandit and scarcity like an armed man" (6:10, 11).

> "One who is slack in his work is brother to one who destroys" (18:9).

> "A sluggard does not plow in season; so at harvest time he looks but finds nothing" (20:4)

> "The sluggard's craving will be the death of him, because his hands refuse to work" (21:25).

> "The sluggard is wiser in his own eyes than seven men who answer discreetly" (26:16).

It isn't hard to see from these verses that the Lord frowns on laziness. Genesis 2:15 reveals that the Lord instituted work from the time of Creation. Therefore, diligence on the job honors Him. Wise King Solomon counseled, "Whatever your hand finds to do, do it with all your might" (Ecclesiastes 9:10). Jesus said, "My Father is always at his work to this very day, and I, too, am working" (John 5:17). The apostle Paul instructed workers to perform their tasks not only when their employers are watching them, "but with sincerity of heart and reverence for the LORD" (Colossians 3:22). "Whatever you do," he continued, "work at it with all your heart, as working for the LORD, not for men, since you know that you will receive an inheritance from the LORD as a reward" (verses 23, 24).

Of course, work requires self-discipline, whether the work involves our discipling mission directly or indirectly. A lack of self-discipline is nothing short of *the subtle sin of intemperance.* Hanging out at the water cooler at the office requires no self-discipline, but it takes self-discipline to hang in there at the desk until the day's tasks are successfully completed. Intemperance persuades us to slump into a recliner rather than jump at the opportunity and challenge to walk across the street to win a neighbor as a friend and recruit him or her as a follower of Jesus. Intemperance finds an excuse to omit daily Bible reading and prayer from our schedule. It leads us to think we could not possibly obey Jesus' commands. Discipling others is an impossible assignment, it tells us. A disciplined mind, on the other hand, assures us that Jesus did not instruct us to disciple others in our own strength or wisdom. It assures us that He possesses "all authority in heaven and on earth" (Matthew 28:18) and has promised to be with us "always, to the very end of the age" (verse 20b).

Athletes at the Olympic Training Center in Colorado Springs value fitness, training, and a sense of purpose. They commit themselves to a strict regimen of exercise, diet, and practice, practice, practice. Under the watchful eyes trainers, coaches, and computers, they monitor their progress, pinpoint their strengths and weaknesses, and adjust their motions and habits so they can perform at the highest possible level. *Go for the gold* is more than a slogan to them; it is their passion!

First-century Olympians, too, followed an intense regimen of diet, exercise, and practice. For 10 months prior to competition they trained vigorously and practiced long and hard. They abstained from wine during this period and eliminated sweets and pleasant food from their diet.

Like Olympic athletes, all who follow Jesus must discipline themselves and keep their focus on the goal of Jesus' approval. *Purposelessness is a subtle sin,* but living to do all and be all that Jesus commanded is a holy endeavor. The apostle Paul didn't compete in Olympic games, but his self-discipline was comparable to that of the best Olympic athletes. He wrote in 1 Corinthians 9:24-27:

> "Do you know that in a race all the runners run, but only one gets the prize? Run in such a way as to get the prize. Everyone who competes in the games goes into strict training. They do it to get a crown that will not last; but we do it to get a crown that will last forever. Therefore I do not run like a man running aimlessly; I do not fight like a man beating the air. No, I beat my body and make it my slave so that after I have preached to others, I myself will not be disqualified for the prize."

It was this sense of purpose and a willingness to practice self-discipline that fortified Paul when he approached martyrdom at the hands of the Roman Empire. He looked back on his years of discipleship as a high adventure. He had carried Jesus' message of love, forgiveness, and hope across the Empire, and he had seen men and women abandon paganism to become Jesus' followers. Now, while awaiting execution, Paul focused on heaven and the reward he would receive there. Writing to Timothy, whom he had discipled in the faith, he testified: "I have fought the good fight, I have finished the race, I have kept the faith. Now there is in store for me the crown of righteousness, which the LORD, the righteous Judge, will award to me on that day—and not only to me, but also to all who have longed for his appearing" (2 Timothy 4:7, 8).

Jesus had called Paul to discipleship in a dramatic way. He appeared to Paul (known as Saul then) when Paul was nearing Damascus, where he planned to apprehend believers, wrap them in chains, and drag them to Jerusalem to be incarcerated. Jesus, the risen Savior, confronted Paul, changed his heart, and commissioned him to disciple the Gentiles. We need not look for an esoteric or extaordinary experience; the Scriptures tell us simply and distinctly to make disciples of all nations (Matthew 28:19). Each of us has the responsibility and privilege, therefore, to obey Jesus and be involved in something grand and eternal. If we refuse to follow Him, ultimately we will step into eternity as big losers (see Mark 8:34-37). The choice is clear. We can choose to *invest* our lives in discipling others, or we can *spend* our lives chasing things that have no eternal value. The words of Francis Bacon should prod us into making the right choice—to make our lives count for eternity. He said: "Here is a test to see if your mission on earth is finished. If you are alive, it isn't."

A performance review is common in business. Once or twice a year a supervisor or manager meets with each employee to discuss his or her job effectiveness and to set new goals. Generally, an employee receives a raise if he or she receives a "meets expectations" or "exceeds expectations" grade. The employee may put this raise toward the purchase of a new car, a vacation trip, paying bills, or something else. Or the employee may choose to invest it by increasing his payday contribution to the company's 401K plan. The choice belongs to the employee. Someday every believer will receive a performance review in heaven. Jesus will conduct this review, and will reward quality service. However, lazy, purposeless Christian living will not be rewarded (1 Corinthians 3:10-15).

In addition to laziness and purposeless, *the subtle sin of indifference* may account for an unrewarded life. Those who shrug their shoulders in response to Jesus' command to make disciples will hang their heads in shame when He conducts a performance review.

Surely the United States can learn from history that indifference to God invites serious consequences. Zechariah, a prophet in Judah about 500 years before Jesus' birth, delivered a stirring message from the Lord. He told the nation of Judah to return to the Lord and complete the construction of the temple as the Lord had commanded. He reminded them that the Lord detested indifference to Him and His Word. He recited the Lord's words to an earlier generation that called for repentance and the implementation of social, moral, and ethical values. "Administer true justice; show mercy and compassion to one another. Do not oppress the widow or the fatherless, the alien or the poor. In your hearts do not think evil of each other," the Lord had commanded that former generation (Zechariah 7:8-10). But the response had been one of indifference; "they made their hearts as hard as flint and would not listen" (verse 12). Consequently, the Lord sent the Babylonians to sweep Judah into captivity (verses 13, 14).

Knowing that America was founded on Judeo-Christian principles, and has always enjoyed blessings beyond those of any other nation, our indifference to Jesus' teachings must be especially obnoxious to God. Do we hear a message of warning and a call to repentance in recent national tragedies? Has our vulnerability persuaded us to cast aside our self-confidence and indifference? Columbine, the bombing of the Murray Federal Building in Oklahoma City, and the attacks on the Pentagon and the World Trade Center send clear signals that our nation needs to be discipled—brought to the acknowledgment that Jesus is Savior and Lord and persuaded to obey Him in all things.

When tragedy strikes the United States, public officials call upon us to pray. National days of prayer follow days of national tragedies. God is "allowed" inside the Washington Beltway, state capitol buildings, and television studios. The day after the "Attack on America," Congress displayed bipartisan unity and took owner-ship of the belief that we need God. The members of Congress stood shoulder to shoulder on the steps of the Capitol, bowed in a moment of silence, and sang "God Bless America." A few days later America observed A Day of Prayer and Remembrance. Crowds gathered on state capitol steps and churches overflowed onto streets. Many who went to church to pray confessed they hadn't stepped inside a church building in years, even decades. Indifference to God took a hike that day!

Lukewarmness is another subtle sin that needs to take a hike. It settles down in our church pews and stares down our pulpits. Just as lukewarm bath water accomplishes nothing and lukewarm drinking water is uninviting, so lukewarm Christianity accomplishes nothing and is uninviting. Yet, a vast number of professing Christians must be lukewarm. How else can we explain the lack of discipling in America? An ABC News/Beliefnet poll revealed that 83 percent of Americans call themselves Christians. According to the survey, 53 percent of Americans are Protestants, 22 percent Catholic, and 8 percent members of other Christian groups. More than one-third (37 percent) of those calling themselves Christians claim they are born-again or evangelical. America does not lack an army of professing Christians but it needs more committed soldiers—men and women who will obey Jesus and carry out their discipling mission.

Many Bible teachers see a parallel between the church today and the church at Laodicea in the first century. Jesus described the Laodicean church as "neither cold nor hot," adding, "I wish you were either one or the other" (Revelation 3:15).

The Laodicean church was smug, complacent, and self-confident. It boasted, "I am rich; I have acquired wealth and do not need a thing" (verse 17a).

But Jesus saw past this lukewarm church's material riches and saw its impoverished spirit. "But you do not realize that you are wretched, pitiful, poor, blind and naked" (verse 17). He was ready to spit this lukewarm church out of His mouth if it refused to see its true condition and repent (verses 16-19). His rebuke included counsel to purchase salve from Him for their eyes. This offer was particularly significant because the city of Laodicea was famous for its production of eye salve.

Have churches in America assumed the characteristics of the Laodicea church? Even one "Laodicean" church within our borders is one too many. But how many congregations are more committed to programs that don't matter than to the Person who really matters? How many reach out to shake one another's hands, but fail to give a helping hand to the community's distressed or homeless? How many get excited about entertainment but excuse themselves from visitation? How many huddle for church potlucks but never help the poor? How many church-goers revere the Bible but seldom read it? How many heads of families say they believe in prayer but never lead their families in prayer? How many churches subscribe to Jesus' command to "love your neighbor as yourself," but cancel their subscription when a neighbor offends them? How many agree that Jesus is the friend of sinners, but refuse to befriend "sinners"? How many want their congregation to grow but only on an our-kind-of-people basis? How many churches have told Jesus essentially, "We don't need anything; we are exceeding our budget; we are loaded with talent; we like things just the way they are; and the thought of making disciples just doesn't appeal to us"?

Whether lukewarmness characterizes a church or an individual, it offends our Lord and must be countered with repentance and renewed commitment to Him.

The subtle sins of lukewarmness, laziness, intemperance, indifference, and purposelessness are symptomatic of sleeping sickness. Those who show these symptoms are sleeping in the Son. They need a wake-up call.

Dr. Vance Havner, an evangelist whose preaching spanned at least 70 years, related the story of an elderly couple with an erratic grandfather clock. It never chimed the right number of times, but one night it disturbed the man of the house more than ever before. He and his wife had retired for the night, but while she slept he tossed about. He heard the clock chime *one, two, three, four.* He counted as he listened. *Five, six, seven, eight.* He continued to count. *Nine, ten, eleven, twelve.* Then the clock chimed *thirteen.* The old man poked his wife in the ribs. "Old gal," you'd better get up," he said. "It's later now than it's ever been before."

All who are sleeping in the Son instead of being alert to opportunities to disciple others must understand that it is later now than it has ever been before. We may not have much more time to disciple our nation. Romans 13:11 issues a wake-up call: "The hour has come for you to wake up from your slumber, because our salvation [Christ's return] is nearer now than when we first believed."

For Personal Reflection and/or Group Discussion

1. How committed to the task of making disciples is the church in the United States? Explain your answer.

2. What do you think it means to "watch and pray"?

3. Do you know someone who is truly a disciple? How does he or she demonstrate what it means to be Jesus' disciple?

4. In your opinion, what are the worst effects of the subtle sin of laziness?

5. In what practical ways might followers of Jesus invest their lives rather than spend them?

6. What do you think it might take to eradicate indifference from the Christian population in America?

7. What might happen in our nation if Christians repented of the subtle sin of indifference?

8. What indications of lukewarmness do you see in the American church?

9. How confident are you that the United States will be discipled in this generation? Why?

10. How does following Jesus make life purposeful?

Chapter 11

IT'S HARD TO WARM UP TO A PORCUPINE

What kind of animal do you most resemble? Perhaps you faced this question before getting hired. You may have been asked, as well, what kind of animal others think you resemble.

The likelihood that you answered either question, "Porcupine," is extremely rare to non-existent. Tiger, beaver, horse, St. Bernard, lion, panda, fox—maybe. But porcupine? No way! Get close to a porcupine, and you may live to regret it. When threatened, a porcupine runs backward into its enemy and strikes with its barbed quills. That can turn anybody's day into a nightmare!

You may never encounter a porcupine, but don't expect to go through life without running into a porcupine-like person occasionally. Rub that person the wrong way, and look out—you may quickly be on the receiving end of some razor-sharp barbs.

The porcupine type may try to hide his or her prickly personality, but sooner or later the "quills" stick out, take aim, strike, and cause pain and suffering. The "quills" are *subtle sins: closed-mindedness, being demanding, dissension, dogmatism, domination, being impatient with people, irritability, inflexibility, a judgmental attitude, rudeness, prejudice, emotional abuse, lack of affection, and a temperamental disposition.* Each one pokes out from the porcupine person's thick skin and must be removed and discarded meticulously, not only for good of potential victims but also for the person's own good.

The subtle sins of closed-mindedness, prejudice, and a judgmental attitude usually cluster together. Closed-mindedness refuses to respect opinions, beliefs, attitudes, and ideas that are different from those held by the closed-minded person. Prejudiced individuals refuse to respect people who are different from them. A judgmental person censures those who think or act differently. In a free nation, citizens must be tolerant of diverse views, accepting of one another, and unwilling to condemn their fellow Americans. However, a nation of tolerant citizens does not have to be a nation of automatons. We don't all have to think alike, look alike, and act alike. We can choose to be tolerant while we are free to be different. In a free nation, everyone has a right to express an opinion, hold a distinct set of beliefs, and act as he or she chooses within the limits of the law. Discussion, debate, and exchange of ideas are the American way; closed-mindedness, prejudice, and a judgmental attitude are the barbaric way.

Followers of Jesus in America enjoy a rich heritage of political and religious freedom. The Bill of Rights guarantees our political and religious freedom, but Jesus guarantees our spiritual freedom. By saving us from our sin, He freed us to obey Him. "If you hold to my teaching," He said, "you are really my disciples. Then you will know the truth, and the truth will set you free" (John 8:31, 32). In this great nation, we have the right to hold to Jesus' teachings as "the truth" and to share those teachings with others while respecting their right to disagree.

Obviously, you don't have to be a rocket scientist to figure out how essential it is to separate truth from falsehood and fabrication. Light does not force its way into a closed mind. Therefore, we must open the Bible daily and study it diligently with open eyes and an open mind.

As we meditate upon the Bible, we will learn to "be quick to listen," and "slow to become angry" (James 1:19). Instead of jumping to conclusions, we will listen attentively to what others say and then either modify or explain our viewpoint lovingly, patiently, and rationally. We will also learn that the Bible opposes prejudice. For example, the Book of James underscores the sin of disrespecting the poor. According to Acts 10:34, 35 "God does not show favoritism but accepts men from every nation who fear him and do what is right." John 3:16 excludes no one from God's incomprehensible love. "For God so loved the world that he gave his one and only Son, that whoever believes in him shall not perish but have eternal life."

A young man in his mid-20s, seeking to know God and find meaning for his life, entered a conservative church one Sunday morning. His long, straggly hair clashed with the neatly trimmed haircuts of those who turned away when he approached them. His hope of finding God in such a judgmental environment had almost faded when the youth pastor greeted him with a bear hug, a smile, and the words, "Hi. I'm Barry. Welcome to our church. Let me introduce you to a few of our people."

Adding to the youth pastor's friendliness, the Williams family invited the young man to sit with them and be their guest for lunch after the church service.

Fortunately, the loving attitude of a few offset the prejudice, closed-mindedness, and judgmental behavior of others. The young man became a follower of Jesus, attends church regularly, and lends a helping hand to whoever needs it.

Inflexibility, another subtle sin, is the offspring of closed-mindedness. When someone closes his mind, he becomes rigid. Unwilling to see a different point of view, the inflexible person stiffens his will, purses his lips, and says something like, "It's my way or the highway"; "It was good enough in the past, and it's good enough now"; "You'll never get me to work with a computer"; "We've never done it that way before"; "I'm fed up with all the changes around here"; "It will never work."

An inflexible person may refuse to face reality. "My mind's made up; don't confuse me with the facts," the inflexible person communicates.

The following anecdote shows how absurd inflexibility can be. On each of several visits to his psychiatrist, a somber patient insisted, "I'm dead."

"You are not dead," the psychiatrist countered repeatedly. "If you were dead, you would not be sitting and talking in my office. Five times a day I want you to stand in front of a mirror and say, 'Dead men don't bleed. Dead men don't bleed. Dead men don't bleed.' Two weeks from today, I want to see you again."

The patient followed instructions perfectly. Two weeks later, he returned to the psychiatrist's office.

"Tell me what you have been saying five times a day in front of a mirror," the psychiatrist asked.

"Dead men don't bleed. Dead men don't bleed, Dead men . . ."

Before the patient could finish the words, the psychiatrist pricked the patient's right index finger with a small needle. Looking at a glob of blood oozing from his finger, the patient exclaimed, "It's amazing. Dead men do bleed."

What would our world be like if everyone were inflexible? Creativity would cease to exist. Business, medical science, technology, and many other cultural enterprises would come to a screeching halt. Our nation's families would experience irreconcilable differences, and our congregations would splinter. We simply can't afford the price of inflexibility. Nor can we ignore the fact that the Lord encourages us to be flexible—to be willing to pursue new ways to communicate His Word to the world, to read and understand the perspectives of a postmodern society and adjust appropriately to its needs, and to trade in antiquated church programs for new ones that further the work of making disciples. Churches must leave the past behind, capture the present, and reach out to the future. Past accomplishments must be guide posts, not hitching posts!

A congregation in the West decided to combine faith and flexibility in a new discipling effort. The Wednesday evening prayer service attended by about 10 would become something quite different. A traditional Wednesday prayer service would remain, but a number of activities matching neighborhood interests would be implemented. The congregation caught the vision, and soon volunteers were on board for a new Wednesday evening discipling opportunity. They would teach their personal skill or craft for 55 minutes, followed by a five-minute devotional.

Flyers were distributed throughout the neighborhood, inviting adults, children, and youth to the church for six weeks of specialized learning, friendship, and a five-minute devotional. Classes included such subjects as ceramics, flower arranging, clowning, and auto mechanics. This willingness on the part of the congregation to be flexible brought an extraordinarily good response. Wednesday evenings came alive with people and discipling opportunities.

We must understand, however that programs alone do not make disciples. Disciples make disciples. Disciples share Jesus' teachings in a positive way verbally and visually. They don't just talk about His teachings; they walk in His teachings. Often, they show most clearly what it means to follow Jesus by being patient with others, kind, loving, and generous. They recognize that the subtle sins we have already identified as well as other subtle sins cause unbelievers to tune out the spoken word about Jesus. Some of these other *subtle sins are irritability, rudeness, domination, dogmatism, emotional abuse, lack of affection, and a temperamental disposition.* A quick review of Jesus' life discloses the fact that none of His words or actions were tainted with these poisonous subtle sins—or any sin at all. He communicated perfect teachings and led a perfect life.

Because we are imperfect, we may exhibit signs of irritability. We may lose our temper at the slightest provocation, snap at our family members, gripe about our employment conditions, or scream at our friends. Those closest to us may despair, supposing that nothing makes us happy and we wear our feelings on our shirtsleeves. Consequently, they feel they are walking on eggshells when they approach us, or they choose to avoid us as often as possible. Sensing that our personalities are less than charming, we may decide to isolate ourselves from others and accuse them of cutting us off. Or we may simply assume we cannot help being the way we are. However, the Bible commands us to be peaceable and considerate and to avoid arguments and quarrels (Titus 3:2, 9). God's Rx for irritability prescribes confession, repentance, and divine love. It also prescribes daily exercises of patience, forgiveness, and kindness.

The subtle sin of rudeness is another stubborn quality that requires corrective action. Left unchecked, it can ruin friendships and alienate potential followers of Jesus. How would you feel if a car displaying a Christian bumper sticker slogan or fish emblem cut you off in traffic? If an irate member of your congregation ridiculed the opinion you expressed in a study group? If someone wearing a JESUS LOVES YOU Tee shirt cut into line ahead of you at the grocery store? If you offered a handshake and a smile to the person sitting next to you at church, but that person snubbed you? If a believer at your restaurant table complained constantly about the food and service and chose not to tip the server? If a letter to the editor resorted to vicious name-calling while extolling Christian values? If a Christian neighbor cranked up his stereo and blasted your eardrums past midnight? These rude behaviors are just a few of the ways some believers alienate others and offend the Lord.

The Bible instructs us to live in harmony with others, to be sympathetic, loving, compassionate, and humble (1 Peter 3:8). In other words, be courteous!

Applying 1 Peter 3:8 to the previous situations, consider how courtesy might persuade others about the genuineness of Christianity and the positive difference Jesus makes in a life. How would you feel if a car displaying a Christian bumper sticker slogan or fish emblem slowed to help you merge into traffic? If a member of your congregation thanked you for the opinion you expressed in a study group?

If someone wearing a JESUS LOVES YOU Tee shirt invited you to get into line ahead of him at the grocery store because you had only a couple of items? If you offered a handshake and a smile to the person sitting next to you at church, and that person responded in kind and gave his name? If a believer at your restaurant table mentioned politely to the server that she had ordered green beans, not pinto beans; and left a generous tip at the end of the meal? If a letter to the editor reflected a loving attitude while extolling Christian values? If a Christian neighbor offered to lower his stereo's volume and not play it past 10:00 P.M. if it disturbed you?

Sadly, even the home, which should offer a preview of heaven, may project a number of *subtle sins, including a demanding attitude, domination, impatience, emotional abuse, a temperamental attitude, and lack of affection.*

Likely, most believers identify a husband and/or father as the Biblically appointed leader of the home (Genesis 3:16; 1 Corinthians 11:3; Ephesians 5:23), a role defined in the Bible as one of love, patience, understanding, gentleness, and spiritual guidance. The following verses make it clear that a demanding attitude, domination, impatience, emotional abuse, a temperamental attitude, and a lack of affection do not match the job qualifications required of the head of a household, whether male or female:

> "A kindhearted woman gains respect" (Proverbs 11:16).

> "Reckless words pierce like a sword, but the tongue of the wise brings healing" (Proverbs 12:18).

> "A patient man has great understanding, but a quick-tempered man displays folly" (Proverbs 14:29).

> "Fathers, do not exasperate your children . . . " (Ephesians 6:4).

> "Husbands, love your wives and do not be harsh with them" (Colossians 3:19).

> "Husbands . . . be considerate as you live with your wives, and treat them with respect as the weaker partner and as heirs with you of the gracious gift of life, so that nothing will hinder your prayers" (1 Peter 3:7).

"Love is patient, love is kind. It does not envy, it does not boast, it is not proud. It is not rude, it is not self-seeking, it is not easily angered. It keeps no record of wrongs . . . it always protects, always trusts, always hopes, always perseveres" (1 Corinthians 13:4-7).

"Husbands, love your wives, just as Christ loved the church and gave himself up for her" (Ephesians 5:25).

The terrorist attacks of September 11, 2001, demonstrated forcefully but horrifically that life is extremely fragile and uncertain. Thousands of families said good-bye to mothers, fathers, sisters, brothers, sons, and daughters in the morning, expecting to see them return in that evening. They could not have known they were saying good-bye for the last time. Their fellow Americans sympathized, dug deeply into their pockets, and contributed generously to efforts aimed at assisting the grieving families. Americans also opened a deeper place in their hearts for their own family members. They told their spouses, children, and grandchildren, "I love you." They called distant siblings and other relatives and assured them of their love. They spoke kindly to neighbors, and joined hands with strangers at memorial services and other public events. A kinder, more loving nation sang with one heart, "America, the Beautiful."

But we should be kind, loving parents, sons and daughters, brothers and sisters in ordinary times as well as in ominous times. We should hold good faith in our hearts instead of ill will. Instead of condemning one another, we should commend one another. Attempts to dominate family members should be replaced by acts of deferring to them. We need to subtract harsh words from our vocabulary and add words that heal and help. We need to stop being impatient with one another and start being patient. We need to expel emotional abuse from our homes and extend unconditional acceptance to every family member. Moodiness or a temperamental spirit should be shown the back door, while we open the front door to reason, self-control, and a pleasant temperament. No follower of Jesus should fit the description one wife applied to her husband: "Kurt is really temperamental. Ninety-five percent temper, and 5 percent mental."

We can learn a valuable lesson from an incident in which a mother asked her six-year-old son what loving kindness is. He replied, "When I ask you for a piece of toast with butter on it and you give it to me, that's kindness. But when you put jelly on it, that's loving kindness."

Jesus, who fed the hungry multitudes, commanded His followers to make disciples. *The subtle sins of closed-mindedness, deception, being demanding, dissension, dogmatism, domination, being impatient with people, irritability, inflexibility, a judgmental attitude, rudeness, prejudice, emotional abuse, lack of affection, and a temperamental disposition* drive the hungry away. If we want to draw the hungry to Jesus, we must repent of these sins, turn from them, rely on the Holy Spirit to renew our minds and refine our spirits and fill us with loving kindness (see Romans 12:2; Galatians 5:22, 23; and Ephesians 4:23).

Let's spread more jelly on the toast!

For Personal Reflection and/or Group Discussion

1. How would you explain the difference between being closed-minded and holding Biblical convictions?

2. What quality do you dislike most in a coworker's personality? Why?

3. What quality do you dislike most in your own personality? Why?

4. Which is harder, to be patient with circumstances or to be patient with people? Why?

5. Why do you agree or disagree that most churches resist change?

6. What are three of your biggest pet peeves? How can you cope with them in a way that honors the Lord?

7. How does a good family life contribute to our nation's well-being?

8. How can a parent discipline his or her children without assuming a dictatorial role?

9. What forms of emotional abuse have you observed? Which of Jesus' teachings oppose emotional abuse?

10. How might an obedient follower of Jesus "spread more jelly on the toast"?

Chapter 12

THE DUMPS ARE TERRIBLE PLACES TO LIVE!

Be positive! Sound advice, isn't it? Counselors advise their counselees to fill their minds with positive thoughts, and many self-help psychology books applaud the power of positive thinking. Management encourages employees to leave all their negative baggage at the entrance and be positive about their work. Coaches deliver pep talks loaded with assurances that the players can win their Division if they maintain a positive attitude. Teachers tell their students to believe in themselves so they can become whatever they dream. Communicators tell us the road to conflict resolution is paved with such positive devices as good listening, complimentary remarks, and generous reinforcement. For example, a husband and wife should resolve every disagreement by stating viewpoints clearly without accusing or insulting the other person, listen carefully without interrupting, reflect the other's statements accurately, focus on the other's good qualities, and be open to change or compromise. Each partner should avoid using negative body language. Tightly folded arms, rolling the eyes, frowns, glares, a furrowed forehead, shaking the head from side to side, and leaning away from the other person inflame hostile feelings.

Even our vocabulary has been affected by the assault on negativity. The word "problems" has been chased from the work-place. What we used to call problems we now call "challenges." The words, "handicap" and "disability" have become politically incorrect. They, too, are now "challenges." Years ago "garbage men picked up our garbage," but a positive spin on life has resulted in "sanitation workers collecting our trash or waste" these days. And it doesn't go to a "dump"; it goes to a "landfill." Landfill sounds a whole lot more positive than dump, don't you agree? It's environmentally friendly too!

Nevertheless, you don't hear a depressed person lament, "I'm feeling down in the landfills today." When someone is depressed, he is down in the dumps no matter how positive our vocabulary may be.

The dumps are terrible places to live; yet millions of Americans live there—at least for a while. *The subtle sins of depression, anxiety, discouragement, or guilt* have evicted them from a peaceful domain and deposited them in the dumps. For many, life has become stark, dismal, gloomy, grim, and even hopeless.

Each year, nearly 17 million Americans develop depression, also known as a mood disorder. Experts agree the figure could be higher because half the people who suffer depression don't report it. Often, a chemical imbalance or some other physiological condition triggers depression, but in some cases depression is nothing less than a subtle sin. Depression usually sends S.O.S. signals such as sadness, unusual sleep patterns, loss of appetite, feelings of hopelessness or worthlessness, weight gain or loss, fatigue for no apparent reason, inability to enjoy life as before, difficulty thinking or concentrating, withdrawal, and thoughts or statements about killing oneself. Medical research has even linked major depression to shrinkage in the brain. In some cases, the hippocampus, a brain region has shrunk nearly 20 percent after prolonged major depression.

Confronting depression is not easy, but it is necessary. A thorough medical examination is a must. However, the possibility exists that one's depression may stem from a broken relationship with God and be accompanied by guilt. In the days of the prophet Isaiah, the Lord called His disobedient people "a brood of rebels" and declared, " . . . the wicked are like the tossing sea, which cannot rest, whose waves cast up mire and mud. There is no peace . . . for the wicked" (Isaiah 57:20, 21). Just as waves heave and roll in the path of a hurricane, so the soul churns and pounds in the wake of rebellion against God.

On the other hand, a right relationship with God calms the heart, soothes the soul, and settles the mind. Isaiah 26:3 affirms, "You will keep in perfect peace him whose mind is steadfast, because he trusts in you." Jesus promised this peace to His followers. "Peace I leave with you; my peace I give you. I do not give to you as the world gives. Do not let your hearts be troubled and do not be afraid" (John 14:27). "Great peace have they who love your law, and nothing can make them stumble," Psalm 119:165 promises.

Psalm 51 unfolds a classic example of how the subtle sins of depression and guilt form an alliance against us if we rebel against God. King David, Israel's most famous king, wrote this psalm about 1,000 years before the birth of Christ. In his youth he had rescued the nation from a perilous situation. The bellicose Philistines had rallied behind the giant Goliath to intimidate and paralyze Israel's army. However, armed with only a slingshot and five smooth stones, David put his confidence in the Lord and challenged Goliath. THUD! The mighty giant hit the dust. But David's faith in the Lord wasn't the foxhole variety. He consistently trusted the Lord—in good times as well as hard times, when he sat at a full table or foraged as a fugitive from his enemies. He proved to be a man after God's own heart (Acts 13:22). Who can read David's Psalm 23 and not sense David's closeness to the Lord? Yet, an ugly episode smeared David's "This Is Your Life." He committed adultery with Bathsheba, the wife of Uriah, one of David's soldiers. After learning that he had impregnated Bathsheba, David arranged for Uriah to be killed in frontline military action. Once Uriah was disposed of, David married Bathsheba. However, David did not dispose of his sin. He concealed it until his depression and guilt crushed his soul, plagued his emotions, and vexed his mind. At this lowest point of his life, David repented, confessed his sin, and urged the Lord to restore the joy of salvation to him. Psalm 51 and a companion passage, Psalm 32:3, 4, capture this experience.

David's sin had distanced him from the Lord; robbed him of joy; overwhelmed him with guilt; made him feel dirty; deprived him of sleep; and caused him to feel worthless. His sadness and sense of guilt turned to joy and relief, however, after he confessed his sin to the Lord. He exulted, "Blessed is he whose transgressions are forgiven, whose sins are covered. Blessed is the man whose sin the LORD does not count against him and in whose spirit is no deceit" (Psalm 32:1, 2). He invited others to join in his restored joy: "Rejoice in the LORD and be glad, you righteous; sing, all you who are upright in heart" (verse 11).

Only God can lift guilt from the heart and mind and instill gladness in its place. His mercy is boundless, and His forgiveness is infinite. Once forgiven, it is pointless—even offensive to God—to live under a cloud of guilt. It is far better to marvel at the completeness of His forgiveness and bask in the sunshine of His vast love.

Although King David's depression and guilt were linked to sin and a broken relationship with the Lord, we must resist the urge to file every case of depression under "S" for Sin. Nothing bites more sharply than a false accusation. You may recall that Job's "comforters" only added to his misery by insisting he was suffering because of some sin in his life.

Mrs. H was happy where she had lived for decades. She enjoyed the dry, sunny climate, familiar surroundings, and the proximity of family members. Then her husband took a job in a big city more than a thousand miles away, where the summers were cloudy and steamy and the winters were harsh. She felt isolated, lonely, and misunderstood. When her health took a turn for the worse and the cause went undetected, she became depressed. The only believers she knew were judgmental. They advised her to "get right with God," and even suggested she might be under demonic assault. Their nagging only made matters worse. Finally, an alert physician ordered a blood test others had neglected to order. It showed an abnormality that often triggers the symptoms Mrs. H was experiencing.

Discouragement is certainly more common than depression, but left unchecked it can derail us from following Jesus consistently and serving Him persistently. Therefore, the Bible treats *the subtle sin of discouragement* aggressively. Isaiah 35:3, 4 instructs, "Strengthen the feeble hands, steady the knees that give way; say to those with fearful hearts, 'Be strong, do not fear.'" Hebrews 12:12 offers similar counsel: "Therefore, strengthen your feeble arms and weak knees." Galatians 6:9 compels the discouraged to keep on and never give up: "Let us not become weary in doing good, for at the proper time we will reap a harvest if we do not give up."

When Prime Minister Winston Churchill rallied the British people for the battles of World War II, he hid no punches. He promised a campaign of blood, sweat, toil, and tears, and vowed to fight on the land, on the sea, and in the air. "We will never surrender," he assured the British. Two fingers held in a "V" for victory sign became Mr. Churchill's trademark. The prime minister's stirring words and victory sign carried the nation through horrendous times. The enemy bombed England's buildings but could not bring down her spirit. The people had every reason to be discouraged, but they rose above discouragement.

Jesus did not promise His followers an easy life either. He predicted that trouble and enmity would dog our steps. "If the world hates you," He said, "keep in mind that it hated me first . . . No servant is greater than his master. If they persecuted me, they will persecute you also" (John 15:18, 20). He also said, "In this world you will have trouble. But take heart! I have overcome the world" (16:33). The task of discipling our nation and protecting it from our evil enemy, Satan, is formidable, but we can signal "V" for Victory.

Maintaining confidence in Jesus and anticipating ultimate victory is critical to overcoming discouragement. Someday Jesus will return to earth as King of kings and Lord of lords. He will judge evil, destroy His foes, and incarcerate Satan (Revelation 19:11—20:3). Pointing to the day of His return, Jesus promised, "Behold, I am coming soon! My reward is with me, and I will give to everyone according to what he has done" (Revelation 22:12).

If you are discouraged because evil seems to triumph over good or because calamities strike innocent people or because no one seems to appreciate you, focus on the inevitability that someday Jesus will vanquish evil, wield a scepter of righteousness, and reward His faithful followers.

A missionary couple returning to America after serving four years in the Amazon Valley anticipated an enthusiastic homecoming at the airport. *Surely,* they thought, *a crowd of relatives and friends will be on hand to welcome us home.* However, when they deplaned, only three close relatives greeted them. Discouragement draped their souls like a thick, dark blanket. But a few minutes later, the missionary wife reflected on heaven, their ultimate destination. "Cheer up, Dear," she whispered to her husband. "We aren't home yet."

Perhaps when you were a child and had finished supper's main course, you heard your mother say, "Keep your fork." Her words signaled that dessert was on the way. To paraphrase words from old song, "Your eyes lit up; and your tummy said 'Howdy.'" At times, life may seem to hand you mush—or liver and onions—but keep your fork: dessert is on the way. Jesus is coming, and He's bringing a reward.

Like discouragement, anxiety is widespread. We worry about our health, our children, our aging parents, our jobs, our security, and our finances. We worry about what others think of us. We worry about surgery. We worry about the stock market. We worry about tomorrow. We even worry about the weather. Such *anxiety is a persistent subtle sin* that must be confronted and replaced with faith. Otherwise, it will dull our relationship with the Lord and paralyze our ability to make disciples. Worry erects roadblocks on the walk of faith and issues the disclaimer, "Professing to be a follower of Jesus does not guarantee freedom from anxiety. Individual results may vary."

Dealing effectively with anxiety requires that we understand how pointless and counterproductive it is. Most of the things we worry about never happen. Wringing the hands and asking, "What if . . . " accomplishes nothing; whereas folding the hands and praying, "Your will be done," results in peace of mind and purposeful living.

Jesus counseled, "Therefore I tell you, do not worry about your life, what you will eat or drink; or about your body, what you will wear. Is not life more important than food, and the body more than clothes? . . . Therefore do not worry about tomorrow, for tomorrow will worry about itself. Each day has enough trouble of its own" (Matthew 6:25, 34).

Although much worrying is irrational, real situations also trigger anxiety. Anxiety followed the Columbine shootings. Parents, students, teachers, administrators, staff, and all concerned citizens realized that what took place at Columbine High School could happen elsewhere. They were right. Similar crimes struck schools in other states.

Anxiety increased after the 9-11-01 terrorist attacks. Fearing further barbarian assaults, many Americans chose not to fly. Car rentals, bus and train fares increased dramatically, while the airline industry lost billions of dollars. Restaurants, hotels, theaters, amusement parks, and tourism also suffered financial losses because anxiety kept so many Americans at home.

Anxiety may strike a patient who learns she has breast cancer, the parent whose daughter or son leaves home to attend a distant college, an employee who gets a pink slip, a widow or widower who faces a lonely future, a member of the military about to engage an enemy, or any number of people in equally stressful situations. These kinds of events happen to believers and unbelievers alike, but believers need not worry. Our wise and loving heavenly Father orchestrates everything for our good (Romans 8:28). His hand controls each trial; His ears are open to our cries for help; His heart beats with compassion; His arms enfold us; and His shoulders bear our burdens.

When the path of life twists and turns and becomes steep and rocky, believers need not feel alone, for the Lord Himself walks alongside and supports us. He counsels: "So do not fear, for I am with you; do not be dismayed, for I am your God, I will strengthen you and help you; I will uphold you with my righteous right hand" (Isaiah 41:10).

The apostles Paul and Peter endured many trials, including the threat of execution. However, their trials sharpened their focus on making disciples and helping them overcome anxiety. Paul wrote that his imprisonment had advanced the cause of Christ even into Caesar's elite guard (Philippians 1:12, 13; 4:22). He urged believers: "Do not be anxious about anything, but in everything, by prayer and petition, with thanksgiving, present your requests to God. And the peace of God, which transcends all understanding, will guard your hearts and your minds in Christ Jesus" (4:5-7). Peter gave similar instructions: "Cast all your anxiety on him because he cares for you" (1 Peter 5:7).

If you feel down in the dumps sometime, try the following prescription. Make two lists, one recording your blessings, the other, your adversities. Read the list of blessings slowly and thoughtfully. Then say something like, "Thank you, Lord, for all these blessings and also for those I forgot to list." Next, read the list of adversities and say something like, "Lord, I cast all my anxiety on You." Finally, read aloud the words of

Romans 8:38, 39: "For I am convinced that neither death nor life, neither angels nor demons, neither the present nor the future, nor any powers, neither height nor depth, nor anything else in all creation, will be able to separate [me] from the love of God that is in Christ Jesus our LORD."

By focusing on your blessings you will counteract *the subtle sin of ingratitude* and assure yourself of God's love. Recounting how much He has done for you in the past and is doing for you in the present will help you trust Him to take care of you in the future.

We all need to understand how to turn stress into a positive. If we view it as an opportunity to turn to the Lord for wisdom, patience, and strength, it will benefit us. The options, therefore, are distinctly clear. We may choose to cave in to adversity or to call upon the Almighty, to break down or to bend down, to be overwhelmed by our problems or overjoyed by His peace.

The author of the following poem knew how to cope with anxiety brought on by stress.

> *We mutter and sputter.*
> *We fume and we spurt.*
> *We mumble and grumble.*
> *Our feelings get hurt.*
> *We can't understand things.*
> *Our vision grows dim,*
> *When all that we need*
> *Is a moment with Him.*
> —Anonymous

No anxious person needs to feel he or she has no one to turn to. Jesus "richly blesses all who call on him" (Romans 10:12). Therefore, Jesus' followers can help the depressed, the discouraged, and the worried by introducing them to Jesus. He invites all who are weary and burdened to come to Him and receive His peace (Matthew 11:28).

But how can we persuade our loved ones, friends, and neighbors to become Jesus' followers? Isn't it true that you can lead a horse to water, but you can't make him drink? Yes, it is true; but what if you feed the horse salt before you lead him to water? His thirst will persuade him to drink!

Jesus identified His followers as the salt of the earth (Matthew 5:13). The peace, confidence, joy, and hope Jesus instills in us can make others thirst for the water of life. Let's show them where to find it!

For Personal Reflection and/or Group Discussion

1. Can you identify anyone in the Bible who experienced depression? How did the Lord help that person recover?

2. In your opinion, should a depressed Christian seek medical help? counseling? prayer support? Explain each response.

3. What do you think are the major causes of depression?

4. If an unbelieving friend told you he or she was depressed, how would you respond?

5. If you were depressed, what would you not want to be told by a so-called friend? Why?

6. What exclusive help is available to a follower of Jesus who encounters adversity?

7. What differences, if any, do you see between being concerned and being worried?

8. What letter grade would you assign to the example of inner peace believers are setting? Explain.

9. What trials has God used to enrich your life?

10. How can you encourage someone today?

OVERCOMING Subtle Sins

PART TWO:
Overcoming Subtle Sins

OVERCOMING Subtle Sins

Chapter 13

CONFESSION IS MORE THAN SAYING "I'M SORRY."

How many pastors in your community are teenagers? None? That's not surprising, is it? Pastoral ministry demands a level of maturity, wisdom, faith, experience, and empathy not yet attained by most teenagers.

Jonathan Edwards was different, though. At 17 he became the pastor of a church in Northampton, Massachusetts, in 1720. A graduate of Yale University at the time, he left an indelible impression on America's soul and conscience that prepared the nation for the War for Independence in 1776, the American Constitution and the Bill of Rights. Heralded as "America's greatest thinker," Jonathan Edwards assumed the presidency of Princeton University in 1758.

Communication experts would undoubtedly assign a low grade to Edwards' preaching style. His sermons' content was excellent, but his delivery was wooden. He read his sermons! But one of Edwards' sermons shook his congregation visibly, and sent revival fires sweeping into every village in New England. What has been called The Great Awakening surged through hearts and homes across the colonies.

No one nodded off or snoozed during Jonathan Edwards' famous sermon. Instead, everyone trembled, feared, and repented as Edwards expounded, "Sinners in the Hands of an Angry God." Pierced to the quick and afraid they might slip into hell at any moment, many listeners gripped the back of the pews in front of them. Confession that day included far more than saying, "I'm sorry"; it included deep contrition, a strong sense of God's hatred of sin, awareness that He judges sin, an urgent desire to repent, and a personal commitment to do what is righteous in His sight.

We should not be surprised that Jonathan Edwards and his wife

Sarah blessed America with a noble progeny. By 1900 it included governors of three states, a law school dean, 30 judges, 65 professors, 66 medical doctors, 100 lawyers, 13 college presidents, a law school dean, a medical school dean, a controller of the U.S. Treasury, and a vice-president of the United States. As the Bible promises: "Blessed is the man who fears the LORD, who finds great delight in his commands. His children will be mighty in the land; the generation of the upright will be blessed" (Psalm 112:1, 2).

No one can guarantee that every God-fearing parent will enjoy a progeny of educators, doctors, lawyers, and elected officials, but we dare not underestimate the profound influence godly parents exert on their children and grandchildren. Roots of righteousness generally produce righteous fruit on every branch of the family tree.

Those who wonder where the present generation is heading ought to remember where it came from. A child learns from her parents not only how to walk but also how to act. If her parents lie, she learns to lie. If they can't get through a day without a "fix," she learns to abuse alcohol and drugs. If they cheat, she learns to cheat. If they hate, she learns to hate. If they disrespect authority, she learns to disrespect authority. If they badmouth Christianity, she learns to badmouth Christianity.

Visit any mall in America any Friday night, and you will see groups of teens hanging out. Although some look neat and modest, some are dressed—or almost undressed—and groomed for shock appeal. A few wear caps or shirts displaying vulgar or profane language. Many kids at the mall converse in Gutterese liberally doused with "Oh, my God." You wonder, *What must their parents be like to allow these kids to dress and talk like that?* Of course, you can hazard a guess and most likely be right.

Fortunately, many moms and dads take their parenting responsibilities seriously. They understand their children want them to be their parents, not their peers. Dad may have wanted to be a football quarterback, but he doesn't try to live his unfilled dream through his son. Mom may have aspired to be a beauty queen, but she doesn't try to fulfill her unrealized dream through her daughter. Wise parents pray that their kids will assume roles in life in which they will use the gifts and talents God has given them. They recognize that their children are God's special creations, not their self-serving clones. They teach them to pray and to obey all that Jesus commanded.

The United States faces an uncertain future because blood-thirsty terrorists threaten our security. The ugly sights of WTC devastation, a damaged Pentagon, and a downed passenger jet in Pennsylvania have been joined by scenes of funerals, unemployment, bio-chemical drills, anti-American demonstrations, most-wanted photos of terrorists, and armed soldiers at our airports. Now, as always, our nation's best defense is God, and our nation's best friend is a parent who teaches his or her child to pray. God promises that the righteous will enjoy security and sustenance, and they will see the eternal king (Isaiah 33:16, 17).

But what message does God have for parents who fail to set a righteous example for their children and avoid prayer as though it were strychnine? For adults who lead a hedonistic lifestyle? For agnostics and atheists? For hypocrites? For the indifferent? For those who have hardened their hearts against Him? He offers a message of forgiveness and hope to those who confess their sins, but the confession must include far more than saying, "I'm sorry."

We gain clear insights into the meaning of confession from passages in 2 Chronicles and Psalm 51. After dedicating a magnificent temple of worship, Solomon received a divine revelation. The Lord told him what course of action Israel should take in the event of drought or famine. He prescribed national contrition, prayer, and repentance—the act of turning to God and abandoning evil. "If my people, who are called by my name, will humble themselves and pray and seek my face and turn from their wicked ways, then will I hear from heaven and will forgive their sin and will heal their land" (2 Chronicles 7:14). Although Americans are not God's chosen people and the United States does not have a covenantal relationship with God, as Israel did, we have enjoyed unprecedented opportunity to know and obey God. Christian literature fills sections of bookstores; Christian programming beams from radio stations and television studios; thousands of churches open their doors every Sunday to welcome worshipers; and faithful believers represent the Lord in every village, town, and city. The call to confession and repentance, therefore, is as clear to us as it was to Israel in the days of King Solomon. If we fail to turn to God, we cannot plead ignorance.

Second Chronicles 30 transports us to a later period in Israel's history, nearly 200 years after Solomon's death. The fierce Assyrians had recently conquered the Northern Kingdom of Israel and were now threatening the Southern Kingdom of Judah. However, Judah's King Hezekiah trusted in the Lord and sent couriers throughout the North and the South to invite everyone to return to the Lord and celebrate the Passover in Jerusalem. The message urged:

> "Return to the LORD . . . that he may return to you . . . . Do not be like your fathers and brothers who were unfaithful to the LORD, so that he made them an object of horror . . . . Do not be stiff-necked, as your fathers were; submit to the LORD. Come to the sanctuary . . . . Serve the LORD your God, so that his fierce anger will turn away from you . . . . for the LORD your God is gracious and compassionate. He will not turn his face from you if you return to him" (verses 6-9).

And now for the rest of the story . . .

Spiritual renewal swept over Judah and Israel like a refreshing rain. An enormous crowd assembled in Jerusalem to celebrate the Feast of Unleavened Bread and the Passover. Single-minded about honoring the Lord, the repentant worshipers worshiped Him, removed pagan altars in and around Jerusalem, and participated in the Feasts. The Lord responded to these acts of repentance and worship by pouring His blessings upon His people. But spiritual renewal did not end when the crowd left Jerusalem. After returning to their respective hometowns, the worshipers obliterated everything associated with their former pagan practices.

Did this national wave of repentance benefit the nation? The answer lies in what happened when Judah's vicious enemy, Assyria. Led by Sennacherib, a mass of Assyrian troops invaded Judah and surrounded Lachish, a city 30 miles southwest of Jerusalem. Then, to add insult to injury, Sennacerib dispatched a haughty, insulting letter to King Hezekiah. In effect it demanded, "Surrender! Don't think that your God will deliver you. When we invaded other nations, they called on their gods for help, but those nations collapsed at our feet. You will meet a similar fate." Hezekiah responded to Sennacerib's letter by spreading it before the Lord in the temple. As he did so, he prayed that the Lord would deliver His people and demonstrate that He alone was the true God. That night, the Lord sent an avenging angel to the Assyrians' camp. By morning, the angel had killed 185,000 Assyrian soldiers, including leaders and officers. Sennacerib and the surviving soldiers rushed home, where Sennacerib's sons killed him as he worshiped his pagan god. (Read 2 Chronicles 32:9-22 and Isaiah 37:9-38.)

An increasing rise in the sale of anti-depressants, tranquilizers, and sleeping pills in the United States seems to indicate many Americans are responding to a shaky present and an uncertain future with fear rather than faith. However, if we confess our sins and turn to God, as Hezekiah and his contemporaries did, surely God will calm our fears and defend our freedom. Psalm 33:12 announces: "Blessed is the nation whose God is the LORD." Proverbs 14:34 promises: "Righteousness exalts a nation, but sin is a disgrace to any people."

Psalm 51 records King David's confession of his adulterous relationship with Bathsheba. As we read this confession, we learn not only the heavy personal toll sin exacts but also what it means to truly confess our sins.

Confession includes a sense of personal guilt. King David used such personal terms as "my transgressions," "my iniquity," and "my sin" (Psalm 51:1, 2). His use of the word "transgressions" shows that he regarded his adultery, deception, and treachery as violations of God's law. The episode involving his affair with Bathsheba and his plot to end her husband's life violated God's specific commands: "You shall not murder" (Exodus 20:13); "You shall not commit adultery" (verse 14); and "You shall not covet your neighbor's wife" (verse 17). His use of the word "sin" shows that he recognized that he had purposely missed the path God had marked out for him. He had no one but himself to blame for the path he had followed. His use of the word "iniquity" shows that he regarded his misdeeds as perversities. These acknowledgements of personal guilt weighed heavily upon David's soul. He told the Lord, "I know my transgressions, and my sin is always before me" (Psalm 51:3).

Admitting personal guilt may not be pleasant, but it is a first step towards forgiveness. If a person waded through a mud hole but refused to believe he needed a bath, he might never get clean. If an unkempt person assumed he was well groomed and refused to look at himself in a mirror, he might never shape up. Soap and water and a mirror do nothing for the person who thinks he is clean and dazzling. Similarly, as long as a person refuses to acknowledge his or her sin and guilt, God's love and forgiveness are untapped.

Why doesn't confession of sin sweep across America? Perhaps, the answer lies in part in a pervasive self-righteous attitude. After all, we are a churchgoing nation with an unrivaled record of charitable giving. We send tons of food and medical supplies— and oodles of money—to underprivileged countries. We stand up and fight for freedom. We enjoy a rich spiritual heritage. Our leaders conclude their speeches with "God bless America." Even our Pledge of Allegiance avows that we are "one nation under God." But none of these factors qualify us for favored status with God. Like everyone else in the world, each American has sinned, is guilty before God, and needs the forgiveness God offers through Jesus Christ (Romans 3:22-24; Ephesians 1:7).

Confession also includes a sense of the seriousness of sin. Do we excuse or trivialize our sins, especially our subtle sins, by insisting "Everybody does it" or "Nobody's perfect" or "No one has the right to judge" or "No harm done"? Has sin become an accepted part of the fabric of our culture? How often do you hear God's name taken in vain, not only in the media but also in public and private conversations? How concerned are you that so many men and women live together out of wedlock? that the stigma of having children out of wedlock has almost disappeared? that many TV programs and movies portray bed hopping as normal and acceptable social behavior? that homosexuality is touted by many as a legitimate sexual preference? that a large number of citizens regard abortion as a woman's right to decide what she will do with her body? that pornography thrives on the Internet and in many of our communities? that gambling commands a vast following? that illegal drugs get into the hands of even elementary-age children?

If we saw our sins as David saw his, personal and national confession and revival would erupt today and the United States would become a discipled nation in this generation.

Confession also includes a sense of accountability to God. King David knew he had sinned against Bathsheba and her husband Uriah. He was aware that he had betrayed the nation's trust. But he trembled most because he had sinned against God. He told God, "Against you, you only, have I sinned and done what is evil in your sight" (Psalm 51:4).

David would have been familiar with the greatest of all God's commands to Israel: "Love the LORD your God with all your heart and with all your soul and with all your strength" (Deuteronomy 6:5). If he had obeyed this command, he would not have tumbled eyes open and headfirst into adultery. Also, he would have been familiar with the command to "love your neighbor as yourself" (Leviticus 19:18), which Jesus identified as the second greatest command (Matthew 22:39). If he had obeyed this command, he would not have plotted Uriah's death.

Alabama Supreme Court Justice Roy Moore faced two federal lawsuits in 2001 aimed at removing a monument of the Ten Commandments he had placed in the lobby of the state's judicial building, but his respect for the Ten Commandments should be applauded. After all, if every citizen honored the Ten Commandments, all criminal activity would cease.

But does God really notice our sins and hold us accountable for them? Yes, He does. Hebrews 4:13 states: "Nothing in all creation is hidden from God's sight. Everything is uncovered and laid bare before the eyes of him to whom we must give account." Romans 14:12 cautions: "So then, each of us will give an account of himself to God." And Revelation 20:11-15 describes a final judgment for all unbelievers. At that time, clear evidence of guilt will confront all who failed to turn from sins and believe on Jesus. We learn from verse 12 that they will be judged "according to what they had done as recorded in the books."

Accountability is not new to any of us. Growing up, we lived under house rules established by our parents. For example, we may have been instructed to complete our homework before watching TV or return home by a certain time or keep our elbows off the table or keep our rooms clean. If we violated the rules, we faced the discipline *du jour!* From kindergarten through high school and college rules governed our behavior. The kindergarten teacher explained, "When I say 'rest time,' please put your mat on the floor and lie down." The fourth-grade teacher said, "Copy these fractions onto your papers and add them." The high school History teacher instructed, "Memorize these important dates. You will be asked for them someday on a pop quiz." The college professor assigned papers and warned, "If you turn in your paper late, you will be penalized one letter grade." So we knew the rules and complied—most of the time. Failure to follow the rules carried unpleasant consequences. Even the workplace has rules. Many of the rules appear in the Employee Handbook; our supervisors or managers hand others down to us verbally. We are expected to arrive at work on time, meet or exceed goals, cooperate with our coworkers, perform each task successfully and in a timely manner, and be considerate of our fellow employees' safety and general well-being. Any violation of rules and policies incurs a penalty. Repeated violations may lead to dismissal.

Furthermore, accountability doesn't stop when we complete our education, move away from Mom and Dad, or leave the job at the close of the workday; it rides with us in our cars and accompanies us everywhere. A red traffic light means stop. "No U-Turn" means No U Turn. "Speed Limit 55" means 55 miles per hour. And "No Left Turn" means no left turn. A motorist driving 50 in a posted school zone may quickly learn from a police officer and a judge that the law holds citizens accountable for their driving habits. Other laws demand that we behave civilly, responsibly, and uprightly. Infractions evoke penalties. Respectful compliance contributes to security and peace, both personal and public.

Since we understand and accept the principle of accountability in everyday life, should we not accept it in our relationship with God? Until King David owned up to the fact that he was accountable to God, distress, discomfort, and dissatisfaction plagued him. When he owned up to that accountability and confessed his sin, divine grace liberated him.

Confession includes an appeal for cleansing. Feeling dirty and soiled by sin, David cried out to the Lord to "blot out my transgressions. Wash away all my iniquity and cleanse me from my sin" (Psalm 51:1, 2). He also prayed, "Cleanse me with hyssop, and I will be clean; wash me, and I will be whiter than snow.... Hide your face from my sins and blot out all my iniquity. Create in me a pure heart, O God" (verses 7-10). Americans play hard and work hard. They aren't afraid to get dirty and sweaty, but they refuse to stay that way. After a game of football or soccer, a round of golf, a set of tennis, or a workout at a gym, participants head for the showers. So do many factory workers after their shift. Soap and water work wonders to cleanse, refresh, and restore the body. Similarly, God's forgiveness works wonders to cleanse our sin, refresh our spirit, and restore us to a joyful and peaceful relationship with Him.

David wanted God to blot out his transgressions (verse 1). The imagery suggests the act of using a sponge to erase a written record. David must have visualized his transgressions as a recorded list of offenses against God. He longed to have the slate erased. You may know that two different kinds of markers are available for writing on a transparency to be shown on an overhead projector. You may select either a permanent marker or a water-soluble marker. A permanent marker's writing and sketches remain, but those applied by a water-soluble marker can be erased with a damp cloth. Fortunately, our sins do not have to remain; God can erase them even more efficiently than a damp cloth erases water-soluble marks from an overhead transparency.

Do you operate a computer? If so, you know how to use the delete option. Picture a document of your sins. How many pages of personal sins make up the document? What would happen if you chose to delete that document? Page after page listing your sins would disappear. When God forgives those who confess their sins, he deletes every sin—and even purges the soul's hard drive!

First John 1:9 promises, "If we confess our sins, he [God] is faithful and just and will forgive our sins and purify us from all unrighteousness." The word translated "confess" comes from two Greek words. One means *the same,* the other means *to say.* Together, they mean *to say the same thing* or *to agree.* In confessing our sins, therefore, we say the same thing God says about our sin— we agree with God about our sin. We perceive, as God does, that our sin is ugly, offensive, guilt producing, and destructive. It destroys our relationship with Him, displays an appalling disregard for Jesus' death on the Cross, steals our peace and joy, enslaves us, deserves His disfavor and punishment, and must cease immediately. Such agreement with God about our sin leads to full and free forgiveness.

When King David confessed his sins, he understood that a change of heart lay at the heart of renewing his relationship with God. "Create in me a pure heart, O God," he pleaded (Psalm 51:10). Later, he affirmed, "The sacrifices of God are a broken spirit; a broken and contrite heart, O God, you will not despise" (verse 17). When the heart is renewed, contrite, and filled with love for God and a desire to obey Him, sinning becomes infrequent and righteousness becomes a lifestyle. What might happen if even several thousand believers in the United States humbled themselves before God, confessed their sins, and experienced a purifying of their hearts? As the acclaimed observed, Dwight L. Moody, remarked more than a century ago, the world has yet to see what God can do through a man or a woman who is fully dedicated to Him.

Confession prepares us for the work of making disciples. A hypocrite rarely, if ever, finds a receptive audience when he or she shares the truth. However, confession, repentance, and renewal enable the follower of Jesus to share the truth sincerely and effectively. David understood that once his own heart was pure he could be used by the Lord to plant the truth in the hearts of others. "Then will I teach transgressors your ways, and sinners will turn back to you," he told the Lord (Psalm 51:13).

A small community in the West burst with pride. It had constructed its first fire station, and the building looked perfect. It sported a red-brick exterior, a spacious and well-designed interior, sparkling windows, big doors, a neat lawn, flowers, a paved driveway, a bright new flag, and even a siren on the roof.

At its dedication, however, an alert citizen observed that one important item was missing. The station lacked a fire truck. The town council had forgotten to purchase one.

More than 350,00 churches in America offer a wide choice for worship. Denominational names may differ, but most churches provide a comfortable environment, a full calendar of events, and an assortment of pleasant personalities. But unless a church includes a plan for making disciples and is actively involved in carrying it out, it resembles the not-so-perfect fire station. Jesus commanded His followers to "go and make disciples" (Matthew 28:19). Constructing and maintaining beautiful, busy church buildings may be commendable, but Jesus established His church to extinguish the fires of immorality and rescue the perishing.

Alarms are ringing loudly in our communities. Now is the time to respond. If we confess our sins, share Jesus' teachings, and demonstrate His love, the United States can be a discipled nation in this generation.

For Personal Reflection and/or Group Discussion

1. What do you think the Bible means when it tells us to fear God?

2. How can you fear God and be on friendly terms with Him at the same time?

3. How would you answer the statement that a God of love would never punish anyone?

4. Does telling "little white lies" qualify as sin that offends God? Explain.

5. What does it mean to "not judge, or you too will be judged"?

6. Why is it inadequate just to tell God "I'm sorry"?

7. How might a believer's unconfessed sins hinder a neighbor from believing on Jesus?

8. How can a righteous and holy God forgive our sins?

9. What would you expect to see happen in our nation if confession of sin were widespread?

10. Is a believer's refusal to make disciples a sin? Why or why not?

Chapter 14

OUR EVER-PRESENT HELPER

Todd had ordered a pre-cut house, which he planned to assemble on his newly acquired lot. However, when the building materials arrived, his feet turned cold and his hands perspired. Piles of coded materials covered the lot, and Todd did not know where to begin. Suddenly he feared that building his dream house might turn into his worst nightmare. But an hour later, a construction foreman stepped onto the property and notified Todd that he represented the pre-cut home manufacturer and was there to guide the construction project. From then until the final nail was driven into Todd's house, the foreman supervised Todd and a team of Todd's friends. He showed them how to build trusses, assemble walls and floors, install a roof, and perform every other function. He even performed quality control by pointing out construction errors before they jeopardized the project's integrity. Having such a knowledgeable and alert on-site helper made all the difference. Instead of risking disaster by taking on the job alone, Todd welcomed the assistance he received and joyfully achieved his goal. It was a happy day when he moved his family into their new home.

Building a strong and secure life of obedience to Jesus Christ may seem like a daunting and unattainable task. Where do we begin? How do we fit the pieces of life together? What happens if we make mistakes—if subtle sins mess us up? How can we possibly fulfill Jesus' commission to make disciples? Like Todd, we may face these questions with cold feet and perspiring hands unless we are aware that Someone is on hand to guide us step by step to a successful completion of the task. That Someone is our Helper, the Holy Spirit.

As Jesus prepared His disciples for His crucifixion, resurrection, and ascension into heaven, He promised to send "another Counselor" to them. This Counselor, He said, would be with His followers forever and would even live in them (see John 14:16, 17). Both words, "another" and "Counselor," are significant. "Counselor" in the original language of the New Testament is *parakletos,* meaning called alongside. Synonyms include *comforter, assistant, legal defense, advocate,* and *helper.* The word "another" means another of the same kind. Jesus promised to send His followers the same kind of Counselor or Helper He had been to them since He first commanded, "Follow me." Further, He identified the Counselor-Helper as the Holy Spirit (verse 26).

A woman approaching 70 had been asking her Christian neighbor, Mrs. B, questions about God and the meaning of life. Perhaps, Mrs. B reasoned, a good sermon will answer many of her questions. So she offered to take her neighbor to church. The neighbor accepted the invitation, accompanied Mrs. B to church, and listened intently to the sermon. It did answer many of her questions. But a few still buzzed in her mind, so she asked the pastor for a few minutes of private conversation. Mrs. B agreed to wait for her neighbor in the foyer.

When the pastor and the inquirer rejoined Mrs. B, the pastor explained that the neighbor had found the answers she needed and had professed personal faith in Jesus.

"I have decided to follow Jesus the rest of my life," the neighbor told Mrs. B.

As the two women exited the church, Mrs. B looked back at the pastor, and with fingers crossed, flashed the here's-hoping-it-works sign.

Because Jesus has called the Holy Spirit to accompany His followers and help us be what He wants us to be and do what He wants us to do, our fate does not depend upon luck. We can succeed because the Holy Spirit is our ever-present Helper!

The Holy Spirit helps us understand the Bible. Jesus told His followers that the Holy Spirit would guide them into all truth (John 16:13). The apostle Paul testified that the Holy Spirit communicates God's thoughts to us by enlightening our minds as we read the Scriptures (see 1 Corinthians 2:9-16). As we read the Bible and meditate on it, we learn what Jesus has commanded, what honors Him, what brings peace and joy to our hearts and homes, what life is all about, what lies ahead for Planet Earth, what prayer accomplishes, what innumerable blessings are ours, and what a glorious destiny awaits us.

Unfortunately, the Bible is foreign to thousands of Americans. Many parents have never read Bible stories to their children. Gideons are restricted from distributing New Testaments in class. Often, teachers misinterpret the principle of separation of church and state. Thinking it bans the Bible from public education, they miss the opportunity to include it in the curriculum as a valuable resource for understanding our nation's history, culture, laws, and literature. Television quiz shows that include Bible questions must keep those questions extremely simple. Although contestants are often well versed in arts and entertainment, science, business, and literature, they frequently can't identify Luke as one of the four Gospels or distinguish between Moses and Noah. Many adults think the Bible is dry, boring, contradictory, and obsolete, when in reality it is refreshing, vibrant, flawless, up to date, and focused on the issues of life. Daniel Webster's perspective on the Bible is especially significant for our post-modern, but perilous, times. He advised: "If we abide by the principles taught in the Bible our country will go on prospering and to prosper, but if we and our posterity neglect its instructions and authority, no man can tell how sudden a catastrophe may overwhelm us and bury our glory in profound obscurity."

We can hope that our nation stands ready to rebound from its downward slide away from the Bible. Encouraging signs suggest it is. The terrorists' murderous attacks of September 11 and subsequent threats of biochemical warfare sparked not only American patriotism but also renewed interest in the Bible. Christians on Capitol Hill reported the emergence of prayer and Bible study groups attended by a number of members of Congress and congressional staff. At the same time, many churches witnessed a 30 percent increase in attendance. If our nation has truly embarked on a discipleship journey, we will, as Daniel Webster said, "go on prospering" and not perish from the earth!

A story reports that a young lady purchased a novel, but threw it behind her living room couch after reading only a couple of chapters. She judged it too boring to bother with. A few weeks later, she dated a young man, who she learned was a writer. Soon, she fell in love with him and later discovered he had authored the book she had tossed behind the couch. Armed with this revelation, she quickly reclaimed the book and started reading it again. This time, her attention was riveted to its pages. She loved the plot, the characters, the settings—everything! She considered it the best book she had ever read. Of course, the book had not changed since her initial reading of only two chapters, but now that she knew and loved the author, everything else had changed.

Those who know and love the Bible's Author enjoy the Bible and discover that it is relevant, riveting, dynamic, practical, and richly rewarding. Each time they open the Bible and open their minds and hearts to its teachings—Jesus' teachings—the Holy Spirit increases their understanding. It's an exciting process!

Followers of Jesus in Afghanistan and other antichristian countries have certainly demonstrated their love for the Bible and its Author. According to Voice of the Martyrs released in the fall of 2001, Afghan Christians meet secretly to study the Bible and to worship. Sometimes they walk three or four days to attend Bible classes in Peshawar or other border towns. Such commitment to Jesus ought to challenge us Americans to heed the call of the Holy Spirit to disciple ourselves, our families, and our fellow Americans.

The Holy Spirit helps us overcome sin. The Biblical story of Noah and the Flood both fascinates and warns all who read it. Noah dared to believe and obey God while the culture dared to defy God. Civilization at the time boasted longevity, and advances in construction, industry, and music. Health, longevity, and a booming population marked the times, but wickedness outpaced everything else (see Genesis 4:17-26; 5:3-32; 6:11, 12). God announced that His Spirit would not "contend with man forever" (Genesis 6:3). However, His Spirit wrestled with the human conscience for an additional 120 years—until everyone except Noah and his family had irrevocably spurned His grace. Then He instructed Noah and his family to board the ark Noah had constructed by divine design, closed the door of the ark, and dispatched a deluge to sweep that wicked civilization into perdition.

Although God promised in Genesis 9:15 that He would never

again send a flood to destroy humanity, He has vowed to punish unrepentant sinners (Luke 13:3; Romans 3:23). Sadly, our generation has not taken this vow seriously. Wickedness commands much of our daily newspaper's space and most of the time allotted to our TV news programs. The picture only worsens with time. Jesus forewarned that civilization in the end times will be so wicked that conditions will parallel those of the civilization that preceded the Flood (Matthew 24:37-39).

How can we reverse this swelling tide of evil? Are education, technology, and a thriving economy cure-alls? None of those qualities saved Noah's generation. Nor will education, prosperity, and advanced technology save America. Only repentance and personal faith in Jesus Christ can save our nation. Fortunately, Jesus has sent the Holy Spirit to "convict the world of guilt in regard to sin . . . in regard to righteousness . . . and in regard to judgment" (John 16:8-11).

When America was engaged in World Wars I and II and the Korean Conflict, our military could usually identify its target. The enemy wore distinct uniforms. The Vietnam War changed traditional warfare. Our military found it extremely difficult to discern the enemy, because it often blended in with the general population. Sometimes those who seemed to be villagers following their daily routine suddenly launched a deadly attack against our soldiers. Today, Americans find it even more difficult—almost impossible—to identify a most dangerous enemy, terrorists. Terrorists blended in with other passengers before taking over the controls of two jets and steering them into the Twin Towers of the World Trade Center. Terrorists blended in with the other passengers aboard the flight that crashed in Pennsylvania. Only alertness and heroism on the part of those who challenged the terrorists kept them from completing their mission of mass destruction. An unseen enemy can mail deadly Anthrax bacteria to American citizens. An undetected enemy can enter our country by stealing across any of our borders. Our government urges us not to let terrorism bully us. So we go about our daily business, while we remain cautious, alert, and ready to report any suspicious activity.

Like terrorism, sins are not always easy to identify until they have harmed us or our loved ones. This is particularly true of our own sins, especially our subtle sins. Gossip looks downright ugly on another's lips, but isn't it kind of cute on ours? We recoil at the boasting of an egoist, but don't we love having our own ego stroked? We decry prejudice, but how do we react when a homeless person tries to engage us in conversation?

How does the Holy Spirit help us identify sin? As we read the Bible, the book He inspired, He teaches us right from wrong. We learn, for example, from Colossians 3:5-9 that the following are wrong: sexual immorality, impurity, lust, evil desires, greed, anger, rage, malice, slander, and filthy language, and lying.

Conscience alone is not a reliable monitor of moral behavior, because conscience acts in accord with the standards and values we have established. A person will feel no pangs of conscience when he steals if stealing is a part of his value system. On the other hand, conscience will trouble the person who perceives stealing as something offensive to his value system. It is not uncommon that a person's value system will change dramatically when he or she becomes a follower of Jesus and begins to adopt His righteous standards. Progressively, the Holy Spirit tunes the new disciple's conscience to righteousness. When the disciple sins, the Holy Spirit uses the enlightened conscience to trouble the disciple and persuade him to confess and forsake the sin.

Truth and morality are hot topics. Pilate's question to Jesus, "What is truth?" resounds in discussion groups and universities, from coffee klatches to corporate headquarters, from barbershops to courtrooms. The popular post-modern response is likely to be, "Whatever you want it to be. Each person must decide for himself what truth is." A similar reply awaits the question, "What is moral? What's wrong for you may be right for me and *vice versa.*" These subjective, elusive answers have been spawned by a don't-judge, relativistic, you're okay—I'm-okay, Biblically illiterate society. The challenge facing Jesus' followers is enormous but not impossible. The Holy Spirit helps us know the truth, share the truth, and lead others to Jesus who is the Truth (John 14:6, 17:17; Acts 1:8).

The Holy Spirit helps us become like Jesus. The abbreviation, "WWJD," appeared on bracelets, sweat bands, T-shirts, key chains, and a variety of other items of jewelry and clothing near the end of the last century. It stood for What Would Jesus Do? And it was especially popular among our nation's Christian youth. Allegedly pro golfer Payne Stewart's young son had given his dad a WWJD bracelet, and Payne was so moved by its message that he decided to become a believer. Although his life ended in a plane crash not long after his life-changing decision, he had become a faithful follower of Jesus. Those who knew Payne best spoke of the positive changes they had seen in his life. They spoke, too, about his deep devotion to the Lord and about his love for his wife and family.

You, too, may value the question, *What would Jesus do?* Like Payne Stewart, you want to follow in Jesus' steps. You want to be like Jesus. Be encouraged, because the Holy Spirit helps every follower of Jesus mature in the likeness of Jesus. Like a master gardener, He produces good fruit in our lives. Galatians 5:22, 23 identifies this fruit as qualities Jesus exhibited in His life and ministry on the earth: "love, joy, peace, patience, kindness, goodness, faithfulness, gentleness and self-control." The Spirit also functions as a master sculptor. Second Corinthians 3:18 describes His ministry as one of progressively conforming Jesus' followers into His image. As He shapes our lives, He looks beyond what we are and sees what we will make of us—a finished work of art. He will not rest or lay down His sculpturing tools until we fully resemble Jesus.

We may think some tools the Holy Spirit uses are heavy or sharp, but they are necessary. We know He convicts us of our sins so we will confess and forsake them. Conviction is a sharp tool. We learn from Romans 8:18-30 that He also uses adversity to chip away the rough edges of our lives and thereby conform us to the image of Jesus. Perhaps adversity is His heaviest tool, but it works wonders. Adversity develops patience. It inclines us toward God. Because of adversity, we pray more ardently and depend more completely on God's grace. Adversity strengthens our hope of Heaven. It also equips us to empathize with others who feel isolated in the crucible of suffering. We can pass along God's comfort and hope to them. We can better represent Jesus because we better understand His sufferings.

A neurosurgeon and a pastor were talking together about the

supernatural peace terminally ill followers of Jesus demonstrate. "Believers approach death calmly," the surgeon commented, "because they know a better life is waiting for them in heaven. But often those who are not believers find it hard to deal with their mortality. They have built their lives around material things, and they know they have to leave everything behind. They have nothing to look forward to."

Someday the Holy Spirit will lay down His tools. At that time, every follower of Jesus will be in heaven. All suffering will be over. Tears will end. Heartache will cease. Unbridled joy and peace will continue forever. Best of all, every believer will be like Jesus Christ (1 John 3:3). This consummation of Christlikeness is what the Holy Spirit inspires us to hope for. Now we are free from the *penalty* of sin; with the Holy Spirit's help we are endeavoring to live free from the *power* of sin; and in heaven we will be free from the *presence* of sin. In the meantime, we can cooperate with the Holy Spirit by discipling ourselves by studying the Scriptures, obeying our Savior, and spending time in prayer.

The Holy Spirit equips us to serve others in the name of Jesus. Remember Todd? He received a shipment of building materials. Every piece was marked for a specific fit in the construction of his new house. Under the guidance of a skilled supervisor, Todd and his friends were able to put each item to good use. The New Testament teaches that the Holy Spirit has supplied every follower of Jesus with what are called "spiritual gifts" (1 Corinthians 12:4-7). Romans 12:3-8 explains that these gifts are varied; we do not all have the same gifts; and each of us should use his or her gift humbly and faithfully. These gifts are designed specifically for the work of making disciples, and therefore fall into two categories: evangelism and edification (Ephesians 4:11-13). Evangelism is that part of discipleship that urges others to become Jesus' followers. Edification is the part of discipleship that helps His followers obey His teachings in all things. Disciple-making is, therefore, a recurring cycle.

As you read the lists of spiritual gifts identified in Romans 12, 1 Corinthians 12, and Ephesians 4, you may be pleasantly surprised to learn that many spiritual gifts operate simply but effectively. They are not showcased; they work behind the scenes. They express themselves as deeds of kindness, help, and encouragement. However, these kinds of spiritual gifts are as important to the task of making disciples as the publicly displayed gifts of preaching and teaching. A tasty bowl of soup delivered in Jesus' name to a convalescing senior is as much an act of discipleship as a well-crafted sermon delivered by a preacher. What counts most is that we employ our spiritual gifts for the benefit of others, as Jesus' obedient servants, and with God's love in our hearts. Love, 1 Corinthians 13:13 teaches, is the greatest gift of all! Unless we wrap and deliver our discipling words and deeds in love, they have no value and are likely to come back to us, stamped "Return to Sender."

Every Sunday morning a young boy in Chicago walked past one church and continued about half a mile until he reached the church where D. L. Moody preached. One Sunday, an elder at the first church asked the boy, "Why do you walk to Moody's church? You could save yourself a long walk if you would attend our church."

"I know that," the boy replied, "but they love kids at Moody's church."

Children, teenagers, and adults in America and around the world are looking for love. As Jesus' followers, we can show them genuine love because "God has poured out his love into our hearts by the Holy Spirit, whom he has given us" (Romans 5:5). It's time to let the reservoir overflow!

For Personal Reflection and/or Group Discussion

1. Do you ever feel overwhelmed by the challenges of following Jesus? How does it help you to know Jesus sent the Holy Spirit to assist you?

2. What challenges are you facing right now that require the Holy Spirit's assistance?

3. Why is a life of following Jesus faithfully not dependent on luck?

4. How would you assess the spiritual tone of life in America today?

5. What opportunities are yours for making disciples?

6. What evidence of the Holy Spirit's ministry do you see in other people's lives? In your own life?

7. How can Americans strengthen themselves spiritually to meet terrorists' threats and activities?

8. How can you improve your personal Bible study and application?

9. What are your spiritual gifts? How can you use them to make disciples?

10. What deeds of love will you show this week in each of the following settings: family, neighborhood, and workplace?

Chapter 15

THE POWER OF SELF-DISCIPLINE

Too bad self-discipline can't be taken daily before breakfast as a time-release capsule! On the other hard, it might be priced so high we would not have the necessary self-discipline to put aside the money to buy a 30-day supply. Could it be that we call some drugs wonder drugs because we wonder how we can afford them?

Of course, self-discipline can't be purchased, but we must acquire it to succeed in any worthwhile endeavor. Simply owning fitness equipment doesn't give anyone flat abs or strong biceps. Having a library of books about weight loss doesn't guarantee an ideal weight. A cabinet full of nutritional supplements cannot benefit the person who fails to use the supplements. Only self-discipline moves a treadmill. Only self-discipline chooses a banana instead of a banana split. And only self-discipline opts for a 30-minute walk instead of a 30-minute sit-com. A couch potato may visualize himself as a robust, trim, energetic, ready-for-action super hero, but visualization without activation is as useless as a camera without film.

Before a basketball player in the NBA steps onto the court for a game, he steps up his self-discipline by training and practicing hard. Self-discipline keeps a player practicing his free throws, defensive moves, field goals, passes, and layups. Five self-disciplined players with average talent are in a better position to win games than five above-average players who lack self-discipline.

Erik Weihenmayer knows what self-discipline is all about. He trained thoroughly for his ascent of Mount Everest, and completed the climb successfully. Furthermore, Erik's feat was unprecedented. He is the first blind person to have completed the climb.

When Jesus assembled His team of disciples in the first century, He selected ordinary men from a variety of vocations. They lacked notoriety, seminary diplomas, political clout, social status, and discipling experience. They were a rag-tag crew, a bunch of hybrid peas from different pods, a collection of loose cannons, and a disorderly dozen. At times they showed an appalling lust for personal prestige, a tendency to shoot from the lip, and unwillingness to accept Jesus' teachings. Nevertheless, under Jesus' mentoring, all but one of these men became obedient and productive followers of Jesus. They learned the lesson of self-discipline slowly, but when they had learned it, they turned the world upside down.

They had learned to love Jesus.

They had learned to obey Jesus.

They had learned to submit their wills to Jesus.

They had learned to overcome temptation.

They had learned to surmount trials.

They had learned to triumph over persecution.

They had learned how to serve others.

They had learned to exercise their spiritual gifts faithfully.

They had learned to value the eternal more than the temporal.

They had learned to stay focused on the goal of making disciples.

The apostle Peter was one of those disciples who learned the value of self-discipline. Not long after joining the Twelve, he proved to be strong-willed, impetuous, bombastic, and impulsive, but eventually he grew strong in faith and rich in self-discipline. Sharing what he had learned by experience, he instructed all subsequent followers of Jesus to be self-controlled (1 Peter 1:13; 4:7; 5:8; 2 Peter 1:6).

Although the apostle Paul was not one of the Twelve who followed Jesus in Galilee and Judea, he, too, learned the value of self-discipline. Self-discipline joined hands with Paul's resolute faith to bolster his commitment to Jesus when persecution, trials, and disappointment buffeted him. Like a bulldozer, Paul plowed through every obstacle and never veered from the course of making disciples. He summoned the Corinthian believers to a similar life of self-discipline (1 Corinthians 9:24-27), and testified to his protégé Timothy that he had fought the good fight, finished the race, and kept the faith (2 Timothy 4:7).

Self-discipline keeps Jesus' followers focused on overcoming sins and making disciples. Before Jesus died and rose again, He prayed that the Father would sanctify His followers (John 17:17). He wanted them—and us—to lead righteous lives. After all, a righteous life, like a lighthouse, shines as a beacon of hope in a dark world. Later, when Jesus commanded His followers to make disciples, He guaranteed His unlimited authority and constant presence (Matthew 28:18-20). Our Lord has neither canceled nor suspended the command to make disciples. Now the responsibility falls to us. But His authority and presence accompany the responsibility, and the Holy Spirit empowers us to walk in righteousness and share Jesus' teachings with others (Acts 1:8; Galatians 5:22-24; Ephesians 5:15-18). Self-discipline checks every tendency to rely on our own resources and persuades us to use eight powerful, Biblical tools for overcoming sin and teaching obedience to all Jesus has commanded. These tools are as follows:

(1) Love. When a young woman falls in love, she thinks often about the object of her love. She wants to please him, and she seizes every opportunity to tell others how wonderful he is. Similarly, her suitor loves her. She occupies his thoughts, receives his attention, and slips into his every conversation. No one has to guess the two love each other.

Nor does anyone have to guess that devoted parents love their children. From the time a baby enters their home, parents sacrifice for him. They willingly accept the responsibilities of feeding, clothing, and caring for him. They endure his crying, teething, growing pains, and piano practice. They empathize with his illnesses and disappointments. They hurt when his soccer team loses, and weep when he sprains an ankle. They struggle to help him be an achiever, and they wince when anyone mistreats him. They proudly share pictures they captured from the time he took his first steps until he walked down a church aisle, arm in arm with his new bride.

No one should have to guess that followers of the Lord love Him. Expressing our love for the Lord should be spontaneous and obvious. Jesus commanded: "Love the Lord your God with all your heart and with all your soul and with all your mind" (Matthew 22:37). He also commanded us to love our neighbor as ourselves (verse 39). This kind of love contrasts sharply with the kind of self-serving physical passion much of Hollywood calls love. It also contrasts sharply with the touchy-feely, sentimental emotion that is worked up by exposure to pop psychology or mood-setting music or tear-jerking stories. The love Jesus commanded is not worked up, but sent down by the Holy Spirit (Romans 5:5), reflected back to the Father in worship and obedience, and spread around to others in kind words and deeds.

Jesus said, "If anyone loves me, he will obey my teaching" (John 14:23). He also said, "Love one another. As I have loved you, so you must love one another. By this all men will know that you are my disciples, if you love one another" (13:34, 35). Love for Jesus and love for sin cannot co-exist in the same heart. Neither can love for others and love for sin co-exist there. If we love the Lord, as we should, we fulfill the first four of the Ten Commandments. If we love others as the final six of the Ten Commandments direct us to do, we fulfill those commandments.

Love is a powerful tool. Loving the Lord, we recoil from such subtle sins as pride, egoism, boastfulness, addiction, covetousness, discouragement, gluttony, haughtiness, immoral fantasies, lukewarmness, materialism, prayerlessness, rebellion, selfishness, self-righteousness, unbelief, ungratefulness, and vanity. Loving others restrains us from such sins as anger, animosity, condemnation, closed mindedness, criticism, deception, emotional abuse, envy, gossip, hatred, irritability, jealousy, lack of affection, prejudice, resentment, rudeness, selfish ambition, and unforgiveness.

(2) Prayer. It has been observed that prayer will keep us from sin or sin will keep us from prayer. By praying we draw near to God;

and the nearer to Him we draw, the farther we move away from sin. But it takes self-discipline to pray. Just before Jesus was betrayed in the Garden of Gethsemane, He appointed three of His disciples, Peter, James, and John, to stay alert and to pray at an appointed location in the garden. Then He went a little farther into the garden and prayed intensely. Later, He returned to the three disciples, and found them sleeping. Rebuking their lack of self-discipline, He asked Peter, "Could you men not keep watch with me for one hour? . . . Watch and pray so that you will not fall into temptation. The spirit is willing, but the body is weak" (Matthew 26:40, 41).

Americans lead busy lives. We work hard and play hard. Our so-called free time is crammed with activities: volunteer work, the kids' soccer practice and music lessons, parent-teacher conferences, shopping, continuing education, committee meetings, *ad nauseum*. We barely have time for our favorite TV programs. We eat fast, drive fast, and talk fast. We can't wait to send or receive a phone call. So we keep our cell phones glued to our ears while we are driving or eating out or shopping or playing golf or sitting in a stadium. Cell phones even make trips to restrooms! We believe in the power of prayer, but who can find time to pray?

Hardly anyone can *find* time to pray, but everyone can *make* time to pray. Many followers of Jesus have committed themselves to a daily routine of setting the alarm clock for a time that permits 15 or 20 minutes of prayer before launching the day's activities. They find that this attention to prayer improves their attitude and disposition, helps them cope with stress, and enables them to overcome subtle sins. Of course, they must resist the temptation to shut off the alarm and return to Slumberland. That's why self-discipline is so essential.

Other followers of Jesus set aside time to pray before plopping into bed. Again, self-discipline is essential. Like Jesus' disciples, they may nod off before a final "Amen."

How would you respond if the President invited you to call him at the White House any time and as often as you wished? An even greater invitation to call at any time has been extended to every follower of Jesus. The Lord has invited us to contact Him "so that we may receive mercy and find grace to help in our time of need" (Hebrews 4:16). If we can make time for a cell phone call, surely we can make time for a prayer call.

Self-discipline will prompt us to seek the Lord's help whenever temptation arises. Instead of panicking, we can pray. "Lord, I feel like tearing into Jay for that stinging remark he leveled at me in the conference room. I need Your help to replace this anger with forgiveness and love." "Lord, give me the strength right now to resist the temptation to lie for the sake of a sale." "I feel so edgy today, Lord. I'm ready to scream at the kids. Please help me overcome this irritability." "Lord, the doctor's report was bad. I'm worried. Help me rely on Your promises and experience Your peace."

(3) Truth. Major battles have been fought and won in America's history, but the most crucial battle predates American history and will not end until time merges with eternity. It is the battle of good versus evil, and the mind is the battlefield.

On the side of evil, Satan, also known as the devil, employs falsehood as his main weapon. He targets the mind and blinds it so a victim struck by falsehood does not see the error of his way and the need to believe in Jesus. The apostle Paul wrote: "The god of this age [Satan] has blinded the minds of unbelievers, so that they cannot see the light of the gospel of the glory of Christ, who is the image of God" (2 Corinthians 4:4). Led by Satan in the kingdom of darkness, unbelievers buy into such falsehoods as atheism, agnosticism, humanism, relativism, nihilism, hedonism, and cultism.

On the side of good, God desires to fill the mind with truth— the Bible. Biblical truth enlightens us, sets us free from the power of evil, and guides us into a righteous life style. Psalm 119:9 queries: "How can a young man keep his way pure?" and answers, "By living according to your word." Verse 11 declares, "I have hidden your word in my heart that I might not sin against you." Verse 105 portrays God's Word as a lamp to our feet and a light to our path." Jesus proclaimed that the truth sets us free (John 8:32). Truth, therefore, shapes our moral judgment, empowers us to do right, and liberates us.

However, we do not learn Biblical truth overnight. Nor can we extract all the Bible's life principles at one sitting. Although we can gain help and insight every time we read the Bible, we will maximize its effectiveness in our lives only by studying it diligently and applying its truth diligently. Psalm 1 links consistent and persistent meditation on Scripture and a fruitful life.

No human being can explain why a parent would try to kill his or her own child. September 2, 2001, a Florida mother shot her 6-year-old to death as he watched television at home. Later, she drove to a church, where she shot her 16-year-old son as he stood outside the building. However, the teenager's Bible absorbed most of the blast. After the incident, a sheriff's deputy remarked, "The Bible certainly saved his life."

The Bible can save numerous lives if Americans accept it as truth and obey it. It can save not only lives but also marriages and families.

(4) Righteousness. Hebrews 1:9 reports a statement spoken by our heavenly Father to His Son Jesus: "You have loved righteousness and hated wickedness." This statement captures the essence of Jesus' life and ministry. He lived a perfect life. Even when he was weak, tired, and hungry, He triumphed over the most insidious temptations the devil could hurl at Him. He never had an evil thought, and He never performed an evil deed. Wherever He went, He healed the sick, comforted the afflicted, befriended the friendless, saved the lost, encouraged the faint, fed the hungry, and gave hope to the hopeless. His Father in heaven announced that He was well pleased with His Son (Matthew 17:5), the rank and file Jewish population heard Jesus gladly (Mark 12:37), and even His enemies could not level a legitimate charge against Him (John 8:46; 18:38).

Although we cannot lead a perfect life, we can follow Jesus' example of loving righteousness and hating wickedness if we practice self-discipline. We must turn a deaf ear to temptation, squelch every evil desire when it brews in our soul, and dismiss every evil thought that enters our mind. As Paul wrote in Titus 2:11 and 12: "For the grace of God that brings salvation has appeared to all men. It teaches us to say 'No' to ungodliness and worldly passions, and to live self-controlled, upright and godly lives in this present age."

How do we say "No" to unrighteousness and worldly passions? How do we conduct our lives in a self-controlled, righteous, and godly manner? The Bible offers the answers:

• First, we should acknowledge that God owns our body and His Spirit dwells there. "Do you not know that your body is the temple of the Holy Spirit, who is in you, whom you have received from God?" the apostle Paul asked the Corinthian believers. He continued, "You are not your own; you were bought at a price. Therefore honor God with your body" (see 1 Corinthians 6:19, 20).

• Second, upon acknowledging that God owns our body, we ought to offer our body as a living sacrifice to Him (Romans 12:1). As His self-disciplined living possessions, we choose to guard our minds from wrong philosophies, immoral thoughts, and evil scheming; we refuse to let our eyes focus on impure images; we keep our tongues and lips from speaking perversely or unkindly; we refrain our hands from stealing and committing violence. And we restrict our feet from paths of wickedness. We yield our body parts to God "as instruments of righteousness" (Romans 6:13). Our minds welcome Jesus' teachings and engage in right thinking; our eyes look at what is wholesome, decent, and pure; our tongues and lips speak what is true, helpful, wise, and uplifting; our hands extend friendship, help, and kindness, and they perform honest, productive tasks; and our feet lead us in the paths of righteousness, perhaps taking us across the street to deliver a meal or mend a fence or share the Good News about Jesus.

• Third, we must live daily under the control of the Spirit. Ephesians 5:18 calls upon Jesus' followers to "be filled with the Spirit." A person filled with fear is controlled by fear. A person filled with rage is controlled by rage. A person filled with good will is controlled by good will. And whoever is filled with the Holy Spirit is controlled by the Spirit. Our lives will reflect righteousness in direct proportion to the measure of the Spirit's control over our thoughts and deeds. However, the Holy Spirit does not force His will on us; we must discipline ourselves to begin each day by depending upon Him to enable us to obey Scripture—to make right decisions and perform good works. Throughout each day, we must make choices that agree with the Holy Spirit's purposes for us. At the close of each day, we must offer personal thanks to God for all He provided that day, including the unfailing assistance of His Spirit. If, at any time, we step away from the Spirit's control and into sin, we should confess our waywardness immediately so God will forgive and reset us in the path of righteousness (1 John 1:9).

The righteous life doesn't spring from an occasional day spent under the Spirit's control; it arises from a life yielded day by day to His control. The Bible characterizes the way of righteousness as a walk in the Spirit (Galatians 5:16), not an occasional step in the Spirit.

(5) Faith. Self-discipline chooses faith over doubt, despair, and destructive behavior. The self-disciplined disciple refuses to charge God with evil when bad things happen to good people. She retains her confidence in Jesus' teaching that God is altogether righteous, wise, loving, and kind. She therefore trusts in Him.

When she faces temptation, the trusting follower of Jesus recalls past victories over sin, thanks the Lord for them, and relies on Him for strength to triumph over temptation again.

New trials bring new opportunities for Jesus' obedient followers to exercise faith. They remember how He sustained and comforted them when adversities struck hard, and they trust Him for the grace and patience to endure the current afflictions. Faith helps them avoid such sins as grumbling, resentment, self-pity, depression, irritability, impatience, negativism, fear, anger, and rebellion.

First-century Roman soldiers often faced enemies who shot flaming arrows at them. So the Romans, who carried large shields overlaid with leather, soaked their shields in water. Flaming arrows that struck the water-soaked shields were promptly extinguished. Ephesians 6:16 builds on this imagery by instructing embattled followers of Jesus to "take up the shield of faith, with which you can extinguish all the flaming arrows of the evil one [Satan]." Just as self-discipline was required so the Roman soldiers would raise their shields and resist the enemy instead of turn away and run or do nothing and experience defeat, so we must exercise the self-discipline required to raise our shields of faith and resist our enemy.

Joan, a devout follower of Jesus, lost her husband to cancer a few years ago. Recently, she received word that one of her two daughters had been diagnosed with brain cancer. The doctors predicted Sharon would die within several months. A few days later, Joan's other daughter underwent extensive and complex back surgery, and Joan's son lost his job due to downsizing. Bad news on top of bad news! But Joan met each announcement with faith, and continues to trust in the Lord as her infinitely wise and loving Savior.

Such faith is duplicated daily around the world, as followers of Jesus turn their cares over to Him. They choose to believe that His power is greater than the power of the evil one and His love transcends every crisis. They have disciplined themselves to use faith as a tool for building a life that withstands even the most horrific temptations and trials.

(6) Obedience. "Follow me," Jesus commanded His disciples (Matthew 4:19). Simple words, aren't they? But following Jesus requires self-discipline. As Jesus said, "No one who puts his hand to the plow and looks back is fit for service in the kingdom of God" (Luke 9:62). Jesus always leads us along the path of righteousness, but the appeal of sin often draws us from the path. Then the Holy Spirit convicts us of our waywardness and restores us to the right path.

The United States' military operates elite units called Special Forces. To get accepted into a Special Forces unit, a candidate must prove that he or she is in top physical condition. Medical examinations, a rigorous daily schedule, and grueling trials weed out all but the best. Every member of the Special Forces learns from the outset that commands are orders to be obeyed, not options to be considered. He or she also learns that following commands to the letter may mean the difference between life and death in combat.

Obedient followers of Jesus function like Special Forces; they know what it means to be so self-disciplined that they put duty ahead of personal desire. They willingly forgo "the pleasures of sin" (Hebrews 11:25) in order to serve Jesus, their Commander-in-Chief. They know that one unguarded moment can play into the enemy's hands. The record shows that even famous followers of Jesus have let down their guard, fallen into sin, and exposed the cause of Christ to a volley of ridicule, skepticism, and criticism.

What if our Special Forces did the unthinkable—refused orders to enter enemy territory? What would we think if they dug in their heels and refused to budge from their secure surroundings? We would be appalled. Where is their self-discipline? we would ask. But are we willing to cut some slack to followers of Jesus (including ourselves?) who fail to leave the secure surroundings of church and home to penetrate communities and nations in order to disciple unbelievers? Clearly, we must discipline ourselves to obey Jesus' command to make disciples of all nations (Matthew 28:18-20). As the apostle James wrote, "Anyone, then, who knows the good he ought to do and doesn't do it, sins" (James 4:17).

Forward, march!

(7) Wisdom. How many knowledgeable men and women live in the United States? More than you can count? Of course! Colleges and universities dispense thousands of degrees annually to students who demonstrated acceptable knowledge of prescribed subject matter. Furthermore, our hospitals, medical offices, businesses, government agencies, and charitable organizations bulge with knowledge. Stay-at-home moms, too, are knowledge-able. They seem to know everything from child psychology to Internet research. Their repertoire of knowledge includes world events and domestic engineering, finance and food preparation, communication and commerce, literature and lip-reading, and a host of other subjects.

A second question: How many wise men and women live in the United States? Fewer than you wish? Apparently, not all knowledgeable people are wise. Knowledge simply accumulates and stores facts, whereas wisdom applies facts in the right way. Jesus taught in Matthew 7:24 that a wise person hears His words (knowledge) and puts them into practice (wisdom).

Again, self-discipline is the key to being wise and not just knowledgeable. A person may have a head full of Bible facts and a heart full of sin. But whoever puts into practice what he has learned from the Bible will experience victory over sin.

Sometimes the wisest course of action is to remove oneself from temptation as quickly as possible. The Book of Genesis reports that the captain of Pharaoh's guard appointed Joseph to manage his household and that the captain's wife tempted Joseph daily to sleep with her. But Joseph resisted her advances. He told her he would not sin against God by betraying his boss's trust. One day, when the two were alone in the house, she grabbed him by his cloak and tried to drag him to bed, but he left the garment in her hand and took off running. Knowledge made him aware that he was in a dangerous situation; wisdom prompted him to flee from it.

Throughout life, each of us will face a variety of tempting situations. If we are self-disciplined followers of Jesus, we will wisely apply Biblical truth in those circumstances. We will flee evil desires and pursue righteousness, faith, love and peace (2 Timothy 2:22).

(8) Work. In prayer Jesus said to His heavenly Father, "I have brought you glory on earth by completing the work you gave me to do" (John 17:4). The work Jesus had completed was that of making 12 disciples. Lovingly and patiently He had invested more than three years in the task of teaching His disciples to obey all His commandments. Our commitment to this same task demands self-discipline, but the reward of doing the Lord's work far outweighs the cost. And keeping our focus on doing what pleases Him keeps our focus off what displeases Him—sin. An idle mind is still the devil's workshop, and idle hands are still his tools.

Centuries ago, Jews who had returned to their homeland from captivity in Babylon began to rebuild Jerusalem's walls. The work was hard and tedious. Rubble was strewn everywhere as the aftermath of the Babylonians' invasion. But Nehemiah, the governor, inspired the workers to see themselves as part of a noble and significant cause. Although hostile forces ridiculed and threatened the workers, the rebuilding effort continued. According to Nehemiah 4:8, "they all plotted together to come and fight against Jerusalem and stir up trouble against it."

Nehemiah reported in verse 9, "But we prayed to our God and posted a guard day and night to meet this threat."

Next, the foes tried to divert the workers by inviting Nehemiah to a summit meeting (Nehemiah 6:2). However, this diversionary tactic failed too. Nehemiah perceived that the adversary was intent on disrupting the work. So he responded with a terse but clear message: "I am carrying on a great project and cannot go down. Why should the work stop while I leave it and go down to you?" (verse 3).

Nothing would make the devil more gleeful than to divert Jesus' disciples from the great work of making disciples. Indeed, if we halted our disciple-making effort for a moment, we would prove to be disobedient to Jesus. Having given the devil a foot in the door, so to speak, we would be vulnerable to his attacks, and we would cave in to a multitude of temptations. Like Nehemiah, we must assume an alert posture and say, "I am carrying on a great project. Why should the work stop?"

America stands in critical need of alert, godly disciple makers. Each of us can play a role in the most significant work ever assigned to human beings. Are you involved?

For Personal Reflection and/or Group Discussion

1. What examples of self-discipline have you seen?

2. What impresses you most about the way Jesus transformed the lives of His disciples?

3. In what areas of life do you still need to exercise self-discipline?

4. Do you think most followers of Jesus need to increase their self-discipline? Why or why not?

5. How can prayer help you avoid sinning?

6. How can a follower of Jesus increase his or her faith?

7. How are self-discipline and the Holy Spirit's control of a believer compatible?

8. Can we choose to love God instead of sin? If so, what helps us make that choice?

9. How do you define knowledge? Wisdom? Can a person be truly wise if he or she knows none of Jesus' teachings? Explain.

10. How can you and other followers of Jesus stay focused on the work of making disciples?

Chapter 16

THE TRULY GOOD LIFE

Aah, the good life! Everybody wants it? But what is it?

A motor home?

A motor home with a boat in tow?

A luxurious motor home with a boat in tow?

A brand-new, luxurious motor home with a boat in tow?

A brand-new, luxurious motor home with a boat in tow, and a private dock?

A brand-new, luxurious motor home with a boat in tow, a private dock, and lots of good fishing?

A brand-new, luxurious motor home with a boat in tow, a private dock, lots of good fishing, and someone to clean and cook the fish?

Etcetera?

A spacious home in the city?

A spacious home in the city and a second home in the mountains?

A spacious home in the city, a second home in the mountains near a ski resort?

A spacious home in the city, a second home in the mountains near a ski resort, and the best packed powder in the world?

A spacious home in the city, a second home in the mountains near a ski resort, the best packed powder in the world, and free access to the slopes?

Etcetera?

Lots of money in the bank?

Lots and lots of money in the bank?

Lots and lots of money in the bank and stocks and bonds?

Lots and lots of money in the bank and productive stocks and bonds?

Lots and lots of money in the bank and highly productive stocks and bonds?

Lots and lots of money in the bank, highly productive stocks and bonds, and a huge monthly cash flow?

Etcetera?

You get the point! It seems it always takes just a little bit more to satisfy the human heart. However, the 9-11-01 terrorist attacks on the United States and the fear of future biological, chemical, and nuclear attacks persuaded millions of Americans not to put so much confidence in material things. They began wondering, *How shall we live?*

When Jesus taught the multitudes in Galilee, no skyscrapers dominated city skylines, nor did the median family income rise higher than one or two pennies a day. If an individual had a place to sleep, a garment to wear, and enough food to keep body and soul together, he was doing well. But the human heart was the same then as it is today. It craved love, peace, happiness, forgiveness, and significance; but it also craved material things. Materialism, after all, knows no class distinction. A poor man may be materialistic, whereas a wealthy man may be spiritual. Materialism is not determined by the amount of money or number of possessions a person has but by the attitude he holds toward money and possessions. Contentment is a virtue. Covetousness is a vice.

Jesus explained what the good life is and what it is not. He stressed that the good life does " not consist in the abundance of . . . possessions" (Luke 12:15). Rather, the good life is found in devoted obedience to Jesus. "Follow me," Jesus said, and He declared that He had come to earth to bestow abundant life on those who heed His call.

"That's just pie in the sky by and by," some say about the life Jesus offers. But all who follow Jesus know that a life of obedience to Him is full, free, and fulfilling. It gets even better as the seasons go marching by, and it will be best when the saints go marching in. So the "pie" isn't in the sky. It is available now, and it is delicious and always fresh. Psalm 34:8 invites, "Taste and see that the LORD is good."

The best part of the truly good life is Jesus' friendship. He said, "You are my friends if you do what I command" (John 15:14). If we obey Jesus, we will walk in close fellowship with Him. Subtle sins will not trip us, and the devil's sales pitch will be ineffective. We will be as content to walk with our Friend, Jesus, as were the two disciples who accompanied Him along the Emmaus Road. They later reflected, "Were not our hearts burning within us while he talked with us on the road and opened the Scriptures to us?" (Luke 24:32). The heartburn they experienced was beneficial. We all need their kind of heartburn!

Those who grew up watching Mr. Rogers on TV came to know him as a friend. They learned important lessons from him about friendship, and they felt that his neighborhood was their neighborhood. Parents felt comfortable allowing their children to spend time every day with Mr. Rogers. They trusted him to impart good values. Today's parents may have to look farther, longer, and harder to find suitable friends for their children. Videos, TV programs, and movies capture kids' attention—and often their loyalty—with violent action heroes, voracious monsters, vile aliens, and voodooistic wizards. But if parents look in the Bible, they will learn about a friend who will never disappoint or fail their children. His name is Jesus, and He said, "Let the little children come to me, and do not hinder them, for the kingdom of God belongs to such as these" (Luke 18:16). Of course the best way for parents to introduce their children to Jesus is to model a life of obedience to Him. Love for Jesus can be caught as well as taught.

To be Jesus' friend, one must know Him personally and obey Him implicitly. Merely professing to know and follow Him is as empty as an exploded balloon. Treasury agents protect the President of the United States, but they also guard our nation's currency. They sniff out phony money and snuff out counterfeiting. They get to know the look and feel of real money so well that they can quickly identify funny money. And most observers can distinguish between genuine disciples and the counterfeit variety. They know genuine disciples practice what they preach—the marks of Jesus' teachings are written all over their lives.

Love tops the list of those marks. *The good life overflows with love,* not the sappy, gushy, touch-feely, one-inch-deep-and-two-inches-wide kind of love but the Christlike kind. This love, imparted by the Holy Spirit to every believer, is two-dimensional. It rises to God, and it reaches to others. It fulfills the two greatest commands: "Love God, and love your neighbor as yourself."

Most Americans want to experience loving relationships. What good is a house with a three-car garage if the occupants bicker and snarl, or give one another the cold-shoulder-I'm not-talking-to-you treatment? Money can build a house, but only love can build a home. A home built on love may need some damage control once in a while, but the damage is usually light and the control minimal. We all know couples that fell in love, got married or chose to live together, but soon fell out of love and went separate ways. Hollywood maintains its image of revolving marriages and seems to live out the square dance call, "Change partners." With the exception of some long-term stable marriages among Hollywood's celebrities, the industry seems to foster an extremely casual attitude toward marriage and a disregard for genuine love. Unfortunately, this attitude jeopardizes the thinking and behavior of thousands of vulnerable kids and teenagers.

How can parents teach their children to recognize and show genuine love? By example and precept. Parents who genuinely love the Lord, each other, and their neighbors set an example their kids will respect and follow. Kids who grow up in a strife-torn family may never learn what real love is, nor will they be able to express such love. Verbal teaching about genuine love can and should support lives that exemplify love, but words without complementary behavior will fall flat.

Moms and dads generally want what's best for their children. However, they may misidentify what is truly best. They may work hard to give their children *a* good life but fail to expose them to *the* good life. Supposing that more is better, parents may work long hours away from home to earn enough money to fill the house, basement, garage, and yard with stuff for the kids. But kids need their parents' presence more than their presents. Interactive video games cannot hug a daughter or toss a ball to a son. An ATV may carry a young teen over rough terrain, but it takes a parent's love to get him over life's rough spots. Designer clothes may help a daughter look good, but only a mother's love can help her be good. The best gift parents can give to their children is the gift of themselves, and the cost of that gift is love.

Further, *the truly good life, the life of obeying Jesus and overcoming subtle sins, is characterized by peace.* Psalm 119:165 affirms, "Great peace have they who love your law, and nothing can make them stumble." Jesus promised, "Peace I leave with you; my peace I give you. Do not let your hearts be troubled and do not be afraid" (John 14:27).

Jesus taught that He is the Good Shepherd (John 10:11). His audience was familiar with shepherds and sheep. They were essential to Palestine's economy and were a part of the landscape. No one had to travel far to find a shepherd tend his flock. The shepherd could be seen walking ahead of his sheep, leading and protecting them. Jesus said His sheep follow Him (verse 27). They enjoy the good life—a life of peace—because He protects them and feeds them. As Psalm 23:1-4 testifies:

> "The Lord is my shepherd, I shall not be in want.
> He makes me lie down in green pastures,
> he leads me beside quiet waters,
> he restores my soul.
> He guides me in paths of righteousness
> For his name's sake.
> Even though I walk
> through the valley of the shadow of death,
> I will fear no evil
> For you are with me;
> Your rod and your staff.
> They comfort me."

Jesus' peace contrasts with the kind of peace nations establish with one another. How many international peace treaties have you seen violated? The peace Jesus gives lasts forever. It withstands the onslaught of personal trials, stock market dives, perilous times, grief, job transitions, political upheaval, long distance moves, and short-tempered bosses. It soothes the soul, calms the mind, quiets the heart, and settles the nerves.

Colorado Springs lies at the foot of Pike's Peak, perhaps

the most famous of Colorado's mountains that top 14,000 feet. Like any fast-growing mid-size city, Colorado Springs has a traffic problem: too many cars and too few adequate roads. Consequently, motorists sometimes get stressed. However, if they choose to look west, they can readily see one of the most peaceful scenes in America. Snowed-cap most of the year, Pike's Peak towers into a deep-blue sky. If motorists are stressed, they simply need to look higher than their immediate circumstances.

The good life Jesus gives His followers lets them look above every stressful situation and glimpse heaven itself. Knowing that nothing disturbs heaven, Jesus' followers can face life on earth confidently and calmly.

The framers of the Constitution endorsed the pursuit of life, liberty, and happiness. They must have selected the word "pursuit" because they could not guarantee life, liberty, and happiness. They saw these rich qualities as attainable but not inevitable. But Jesus guarantees all three to those who believe on Him. "I give them eternal life," He said (John 10:27). He promised, " . . . if the Son sets you free, you will be free indeed" (8:36). Also, He assured, "Now that you know these things, you will be blessed [happy] if you do them" (John 13:17).

Happiness is indeed associated with the good life, but did you notice that Jesus linked it to obedience? Simply knowing Jesus' commandments cannot make us happy; we must carry them out. If we obey Jesus, we will be happy even when our circumstances look bleak. We will discover that true happiness does not depend on pleasant happenstances but on persistent loyalty to our Master.

If happiness depended on pleasant happenstances, the apostle Paul would have been one of the unhappiest people of the first century. The circumstances he experienced for the sake of discipling others pummeled him like baseball-size hail. In 2 Corinthians 11:23-33 he listed some of them:

- frequent imprisonment;
- severe flogging;
- imminent death on several occasions;
- lashed with a whip 39 times on five occasions;
- beaten with rods on three occasions;
- stoning;

- shipwreck;
- adrift at sea;
- hounded and hunted by bandits, his own countrymen, false teachers, and Gentiles;
- treacherous rivers, hostile cities, perilous terrain, and dangerous sea crossings;
- exhausting toil;
- sleepless nights;
- hunger;
- thirst;
- food deprivation;
- cold;
- lack of clothing;
- a contract on his life;
- a harrowing escape over a city's wall.

Nevertheless, through all these circumstances Paul possessed a joy that belongs only to those who serve Jesus. Paul was not only *intent* on making disciples in obedience to Jesus' command to do so, but also *content* as he did so. His most prominent words in Philippians, a letter he wrote from prison, are "rejoice," "joy," and "glad."

Forgiveness is another quality associated with the good life Jesus offers. He gained our forgiveness by dying on the cross, and He grants us forgiveness when we believe on Him. The apostle Peter told a Roman centurion and those gathered in Cornelius's house that everyone who believes in Jesus "receives forgiveness of sins through his name" (Acts 10:43).

A grouchy old man examined his photo proofs at a photographer's studio. Years of scowling and furrowing his brow had given the old man gnarled and wrinkled facial features. "These photos don't do me justice," he snapped at the photographer.

"Sir," the photographer replied, "you don't need justice. You need mercy."

When we see ourselves as the Bible pictures us, we realize we need mercy. But we also find good news: God extends mercy to us. Forgiveness is available through Jesus Christ. We gain an immediate release from all our guilt and a new lease on life.

At the height of the Anthrax scare, Colorado Governor Bill Owens received a suspicious envelope containing a white powder and a threatening letter. A return address showed that an inmate had mailed the envelope and contents to the Governor. Upon examination, the white powder turned out to be soap powder. Governor Owens later referred to the incident at a news conference. "I don't think I will be pardoning him any time soon," he quipped.

Forgiveness under such dreadful circumstances would be inconceivable. No one could predict what future crimes the inmate might commit. It is also inconceivable that God would forgive sinners, but He does so. And along with His forgiveness He bestows the motivation and power to turn away from wrongdoing and to walk in righteousness (Romans 8:1-4).

Jesus related the story of the prodigal son so we might have a better understanding of God's amazing forgiveness. The story concerns a young man who took his cash inheritance, blew it on sinful pleasures in a distant place, and ended up by slopping hogs for scarcely survival pay. Then he got smart. He decided to return home, confess the error of his ways, seek Dad's forgiveness and ask him to take him on as a hired hand. However, as he approached his former home, an awesome event transpired. His father ran to him, threw his arms around him, and kissed him.

But that was not the end of the story. The father instructed his servants to outfit his son with the best robe, put a ring on his finger, sandals on his feet, and prepare a festive meal. The forgiving father planned to celebrate his son's return.

No matter how far astray a person has wandered, he or she can come home to a loving heavenly Father's arms. His forgiveness is as unlimited as it is undeserved.

A motel chain invites travelers to stay at any of its locations. The chain offers inexpensive but comfortable accommodations and promises, "We'll leave a light on for you."

God invites sinners to come home, and He leaves a light on— a light that emanates from the righteous lives of Jesus' followers (Matthew 5:14-16).

The good life, the life of following Jesus and overcoming subtle sins, also holds unrivaled significance. Those who obey Jesus know clearly what their life mission is. They discover that serving is more thrilling than sinning. They find that investing their lives in making disciples pays far greater dividends than spending their lives in the pursuit of pleasure.

The apostle Paul's first letter to believers in the Greek city of Corinth includes a challenging paragraph about building a quality life. The paragraph compares the building of a life to that of building a structure. In ancient times a contractor could choose to use cheap, flammable building materials or expensive, durable materials. When a devastating fire swept through Corinth a century and a half before the birth of Christ, structures built of wood, hay or straw burned to the ground. Only structures built with gold, silver, and costly stones remained. Similarly, in any period of history a man or woman may choose to construct a life using either perishable or durable materials. Living in the rebuilt city of Corinth, the recipients of Paul's letter would readily identify with Paul's words about building materials and the test of fire.

Paul told the Corinthians that every believer's works will be tested by fire someday. A life of obedience to Jesus will pass the test and be rewarded, but a life of squandered opportunities will experience loss (see 1 Corinthians 3:10-15).

Early shoppers in a department store were surprised to find low prices on valuable items and high prices on common items. Someone had switched the price tags during the night.

Satan has worked long and hard to switch price tags. He has persuaded the unsuspecting to spend enormous amounts of time, money, and energy for items that can neither last nor offer a sense of fulfillment. In the meantime he has duped many men and women into thinking eternal values are worth little. However, someday it will be clear to all that he has switched the price tags.

The Peace Corps, established by John F. Kennedy, pays very little, but it attracts some of the brightest, most talented, and best-educated youth in our nation. The young men and women who join the Peace Corps are idealistic and altruistic. They believe serving others is the key to building a significant life. The same belief underlies a life of loyal service to Jesus.

Jesus challenged a rich, young ruler to sell his possessions, give the proceeds to the poor, and follow Him. He promised the young man, "You will have treasure in heaven" (Mark 10:21). Unfortunately, the young man put a higher price tag on material things than on service. He rejected Jesus' challenge, and forfeited a truly significant life on earth and treasure in heaven.

A story relates that a king paid a surprise visit to several village stores in his kingdom. He found one shop in total disarray. Clutter filled every corner, and merchandise dangled from every shelf. "I will not tell you the day or hour when I plan to return to your shop," he told the storeowner, "but I promise to return. If I find your store neat and clean and helpful to customers, I will reward you with an 'Approved by the King' sign for display in your window."

No one can say when Jesus, the King of kings, will return. Although many writers and ministers interpret cataclysmic current events as signals that He is coming soon, He did not signify the date or hour of His return. He did promise, however, "Behold, I am coming soon! My reward is with me." He holds the time of His return in His hands, but He has committed the task of preparing for His return in our hands. Our task is to overcome subtle sins and make disciples of all nations. Will we receive an "Approved by the King" reward?

In summary, the good life consists of overcoming sins, obeying Jesus, living our faith, and enjoying His rewards—both now and throughout eternity. Regret and remorse will hound us if we fail to become Jesus' obedient disciples, but we will never be sorry

> for telling the truth;
>
> for living a pure life;
>
> for our faith in Christ;
>
> for confessing our sins;
>
> for doing our best;
>
> for thinking before acting;
>
> for listening before judging;
>
> for forgiving our enemies;
>
> for helping a fallen brother;
>
> for being honest in business;

for thinking before speaking;

for standing by our principles;

for closing our ears to gossip;

for bridling a slanderous tongue;

for harboring only pure thoughts;

for sympathizing with the afflicted;

for being courteous and kind to all;

for giving to the Lord's work.

—Author unknown

For Personal Reflection and/or Group Discussion

1. What do you believe most Americans want most?

2. Do you believe their priority is correct or incorrect? Why?

3. In six words or less identify what you believe is the good life.

4. Where do you think true happiness can be found? Explain your choice.

5. What do you think children want most from their parents?

6. Do you think most parents are giving their children what they want most? Explain.

7. How have you experienced peace in the midst of adversity?

8. What rewards does Jesus give now to those who obey Him?

9. What rewards will Jesus give in heaven to those who obey Him?

10. Identify a few items of little value that many people consider highly valuable. Also, identify a few highly valuable items that many people think have little or no value. How can you help others appreciate what is truly valuable?

*"A disciple is an obedient follower
of Jesus Christ who is actively engaged
in making disciples by teaching obedience
to everything Jesus commanded
in self, family, congregation,
and neighborhood."*